PANORAMA
A HISTORY OF
BUILDINGS
FROM HUTS *TO* HIGHRISE

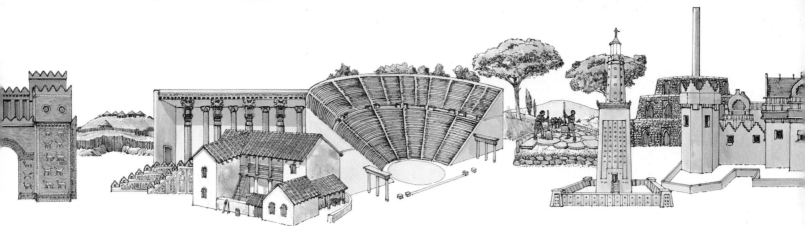

Author:
Fiona Macdonald studied history at
Cambridge University and at the
University of East Anglia, where she is a
part-time tutor in Medieval History. She
has also taught in schools and adult
education and is the author of numerous
books for children on historical subjects,
including *Roman Fort, Viking Town,
Medieval Castle, 16th-Century Mosque* and
19th-Century Railway Station in the **Inside
Story** series.

Series designer:
David Salariya was born in Dundee,
Scotland, where he studied illustration
and printmaking, concentrating on book
design in his post-graduate year. He later
completed a further post-graduate course
in art education at Sussex University. He
has illustrated a wide range of books on
botanical, historical and mythical
subjects. He has designed and created
many new series of children's books for
publishers in the UK and overseas,
including the award-winning **Inside Story**
series. He lives in Brighton with his wife,
the illustrator Shirley Willis.

Illustrations by:
David Antram 14-15, 20-21, 22-23, 24-25, 38-
39, 42-43; **Nick Hewetson** 16-17, 26-27, 36-
37, 40-41; **John James** 10-11, 28-29, 30-31;
Mark Peppé 8-9; **Gerald Wood** 12-13, 18-19,
32-33, 34-35.

Series designer:	David Salariya
Editor:	Penny Clarke
Artists:	David Antram
	Nick Hewetson
	John James
	Mark Peppé
	Gerald Wood

First published in 1996
by Macdonald Young Books
61 Western Road
Hove
East Sussex
BN3 1JD

ISBN 0-7500-1749-X

© The Salariya Book Co Ltd MCMXCVI

Printed in Portugal by Ediçoes ASA

A CIP catalogue record for this book is available from
the British Library title page copy

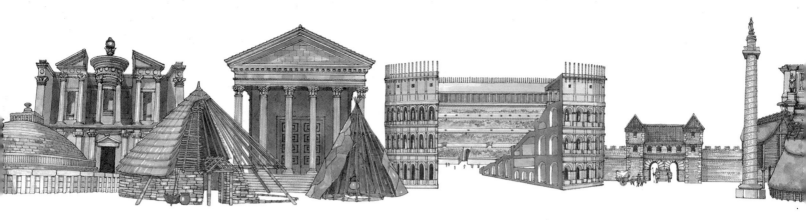

PANORAMA

A HISTORY *OF*

BUILDINGS

FROM HUTS *TO* HIGHRISE

Written by
FIONA MACDONALD

Created & Designed by
DAVID SALARIYA

MACDONALD YOUNG BOOKS

Contents

6 INTRODUCTION

8 PREHISTORIC TIMES
Caves, huts, tents and sun-baked bricks. The first towns.

10 EGYPT AND NEARBY LANDS
Pyramids and ritual baths. Stonehenge and King Solomon's temple.

12 THE GREEK WORLD
Massive walls and gates, hill-forts, stone pillars and burial mounds. The Acropolis at Athens and Alexandria's lighthouse.

14 THE ROMAN WORLD
Villas, farms, triumphal arches and the world's first blocks of flats.

16 AFTER ROME
Hindu temples, sunken houses, great gates. Churches in Africa and Constantinople.

18 THE END OF THE MILLENNIUM
Mosques and places of prayer. Temple pyramids in Mexico. Farming villages and a king's palace.

20 THE EARLY MIDDLE AGES
Buddhist shrines, Russian churches, Chinese bridges. Cathedrals, monasteries and temple cities.

22 THE HIGH MIDDLE AGES
Castles, keeps and curtain walls. Enormous barns. Caravanserais, trading cities and Sainte Chapelle.

24 THE LATE MIDDLE AGES
A synagogue, a Spanish palace, a Javanese temple and a palace for the popes. The Golden Pavilion and the Leaning Tower of Pisa. Great Zimbabwe.

26 THE RENAISSANCE WORLD
London's Guildhall and Moscow's Kremlin. Great Renaissance buildings in Italy.

28 THE 16TH CENTURY
Hampton Court Palace, Longleat and the Louvre. The Escorial and the Globe theatre. The Suleymaniye mosque and the ruins at Vijayanagar.

30 THE 17TH CENTURY
Samurai castles, the Banqueting House and new St Paul's. The splendour of Versailles.

32 THE 18TH CENTURY
The Red Fort, the Belvedere, Melk Abbey and the Temple of Heaven. St Petersburg, the Pantheon and a cast-iron bridge.

34 THE EARLY 19TH CENTURY
The Arc de Triomphe, the White House, Brighton Pavilion and a slave plantation. An arms factory and a pioneer home.

36 THE LATE 19TH CENTURY
Crystal Palace, the Paris Opera and the Clifton suspension bridge. Railway stations, department stores, the Statue of Liberty and the Eiffel Tower.

38 THE EARLY 20TH CENTURY
Buildings in metal, concrete and glass. The Bauhaus, Art Deco and Modern Style. Suburban nostalgia and garden cities.

40 THE MID 20TH CENTURY
New materials, futuristic styles, prefabrication and experimentation. The building as a machine.

42 THE 1960S TO THE PRESENT
Exciting high-tech or brutally ugly? Post-modern skyscrapers and a return to tents.

44 BUILDING FACTS

45 SOME IMPORTANT ARCHITECTS BORN BEFORE 1900

46 GLOSSARY

48 INDEX

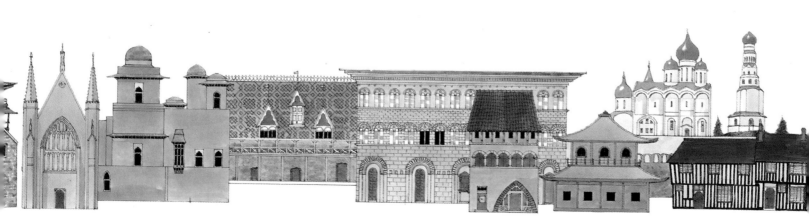

INTRODUCTION

Why are buildings made? First and foremost, to provide shelter from the weather. But buildings are more than just useful. All round the world, and from many different centuries, we find buildings that have been designed to meet many different needs. Buildings can be dramatic, spectacular, beautiful, intriguing, fashionable, holy, mysterious, plain, boring or decidedly odd. There are examples of all these in the following pages.

This book is arranged in date order, from the

earliest-known buildings of around 350,000 BC to the present. Some dates are precise, others are approximate. It is easy to date modern buildings; we know exactly when they were made. But it is far more difficult to date with certainty many buildings that have survived from the past. Sometimes there is no written evidence to give us precise information. Or perhaps a building took a hundred or more years to complete. Another reason may be that there have been several buildings, all with the same name, one after the other on the same site. And many buildings have had new sections added to them, many years after they were first designed.

c10,000 BC

c5000 BC

c35,000-10,000 BC

PREHISTORIC TIMES

Before people started making shelters, they used caves.

We do not

know the names of the first builders, or what gave them the idea of arranging branches to make shelters. It probably developed from peoples' habit of sheltering under trees. Huts were often built inside caves or under overhanging cliffs, for protection from the weather and from enemy attack.

Slowly, over the centuries, builders began to make larger, more elaborate homes. Sometimes animal skins were draped over the branches to make the shelters more weatherproof. Some permanent huts were built over shallow pits, reducing the draughts whistling through cracks where the walls met the ground. Huts might be thatched with leaves or straw. And, although they had no really waterproof materials, builders discovered that a steeply-sloping roof could keep a hut dry inside. If the pitch was steep enough, rainwater would run off and not seep through.

Building huts required very simple technology – cutting and shaping tools of flint and bone. A major building breakthrough came around 8000 BC with the discovery of how to use a common everyday material: mud. Sun-dried mud bricks were used to build houses, palaces and temples in the first towns.

THE EARLIEST-KNOWN buildings (c350,000 BC, from Africa) were simple shelters, made of brushwood.

THE FIRST BUILDERS used simple tools, like this pick made from a deer's antler. Other digging tools were made from sharpened rib bones.

HUT made of wooden poles, c300,000 BC, reconstructed from remains found in southern France.

HUNTERS killed wild animals (mammoth, deer, bison) using bone spear-tips and arrows like these.

entrance in roof

strong walls made of mud brick

c5000-4600 BC

c2800 BC

c4000 BC

c5000 BC

INSIDE a shrine at Çatal Hüyuk where a mother-goddess was worshipped by priestesses wearing cloaks of vulture feathers. A replica bull's skull hung on the wall.

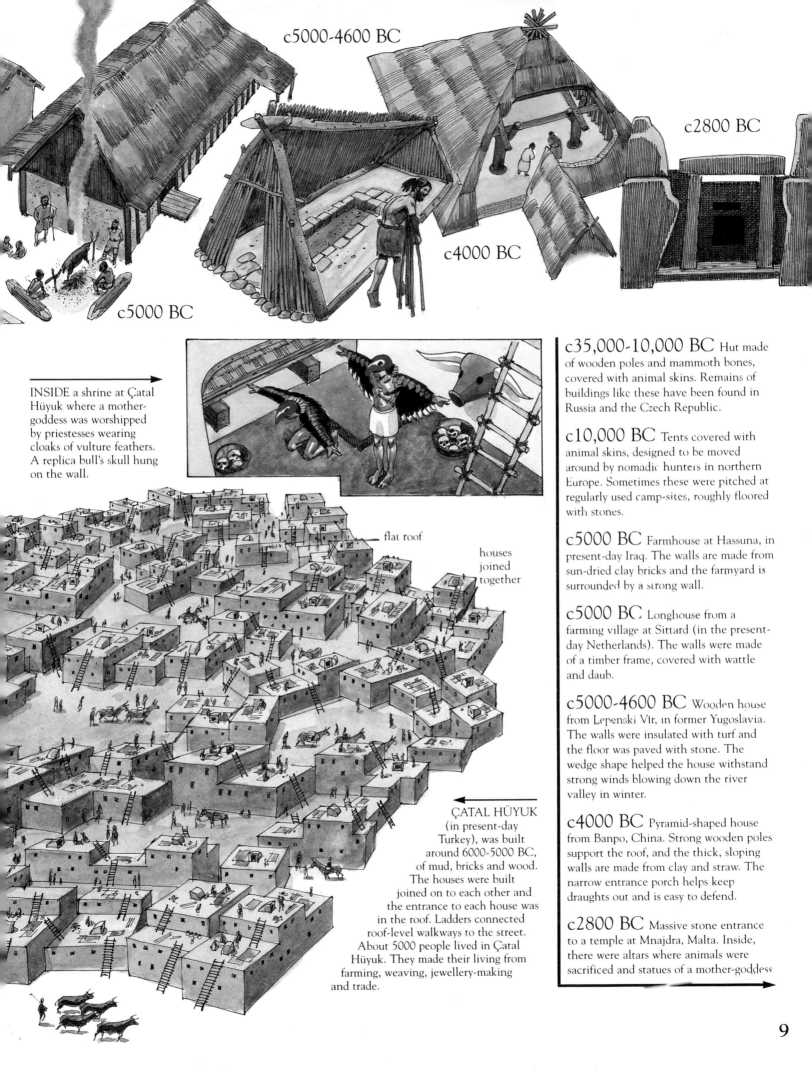

flat roof

houses joined together

ÇATAL HÜYUK (in present-day Turkey), was built around 6000-5000 BC, of mud, bricks and wood. The houses were built joined on to each other and the entrance to each house was in the roof. Ladders connected roof-level walkways to the street. About 5000 people lived in Çatal Hüyuk. They made their living from farming, weaving, jewellery-making and trade.

c35,000-10,000 BC Hut made of wooden poles and mammoth bones, covered with animal skins. Remains of buildings like these have been found in Russia and the Czech Republic.

c10,000 BC Tents covered with animal skins, designed to be moved around by nomadic hunters in northern Europe. Sometimes these were pitched at regularly used camp-sites, roughly floored with stones.

c5000 BC Farmhouse at Hassuna, in present-day Iraq. The walls are made from sun-dried clay bricks and the farmyard is surrounded by a strong wall.

c5000 BC Longhouse from a farming village at Sittard (in the present-day Netherlands). The walls were made of a timber frame, covered with wattle and daub.

c5000-4600 BC Wooden house from Lepenski Vir, in former Yugoslavia. The walls were insulated with turf and the floor was paved with stone. The wedge shape helped the house withstand strong winds blowing down the river valley in winter.

c4000 BC Pyramid-shaped house from Banpo, China. Strong wooden poles support the roof, and the thick, sloping walls are made from clay and straw. The narrow entrance porch helps keep draughts out and is easy to defend.

c2800 BC Massive stone entrance to a temple at Mnajdra, Malta. Inside, there were altars where animals were sacrificed and statues of a mother-goddess

c2650 BC   c2500 BC   c2100 BC   c2000-1700 BC

EGYPT AND NEARBY LANDS

The step-pyramid of King Djoser in Egypt. The first monumental stone building in the world, completed c2680 BC.

↑ THE Temple of Ramesses II (ruled 1290-1224 BC) at Abu Simbel, Egypt.

↑ HOUSE for a scribe and his family, built in Deir el Medinah, Egypt, about 3500 years ago.

Egypt was a fortunate land. For over 2000 years, pharaohs ruled over a prosperous civilization, which drew its wealth from plentiful food crops watered by the River Nile. Egypt also had ample supplies of building stone, as well as educated architects and engineers who had discovered how to work it. The pharaoh's officials were able to command an almost limitless supply of labourers, too.

Egyptian building technology was simple but efficient. There were no big machines, but builders used levers, pulleys and rollers to make the best possible use of human muscle-power.

To the Egyptians, pharaohs were more than ordinary men – they were living representatives of the gods. It seemed only natural, therefore, that the buildings constructed for them should be of superhuman size and splendour. From pyramids to palaces, temples to tombs, Egyptian royal architecture was designed to impress.

Rulers in other lands also built palaces and tombs to reflect their own magnificence, huge temples to show their kinship with the gods. Often, these buildings were sited on artificial mounds, to make them nearer to the heavens.

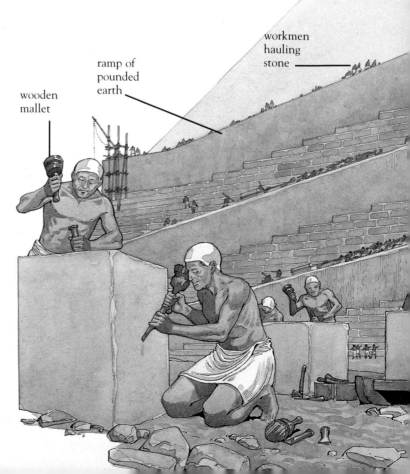

workmen hauling stone

ramp of pounded earth

wooden mallet

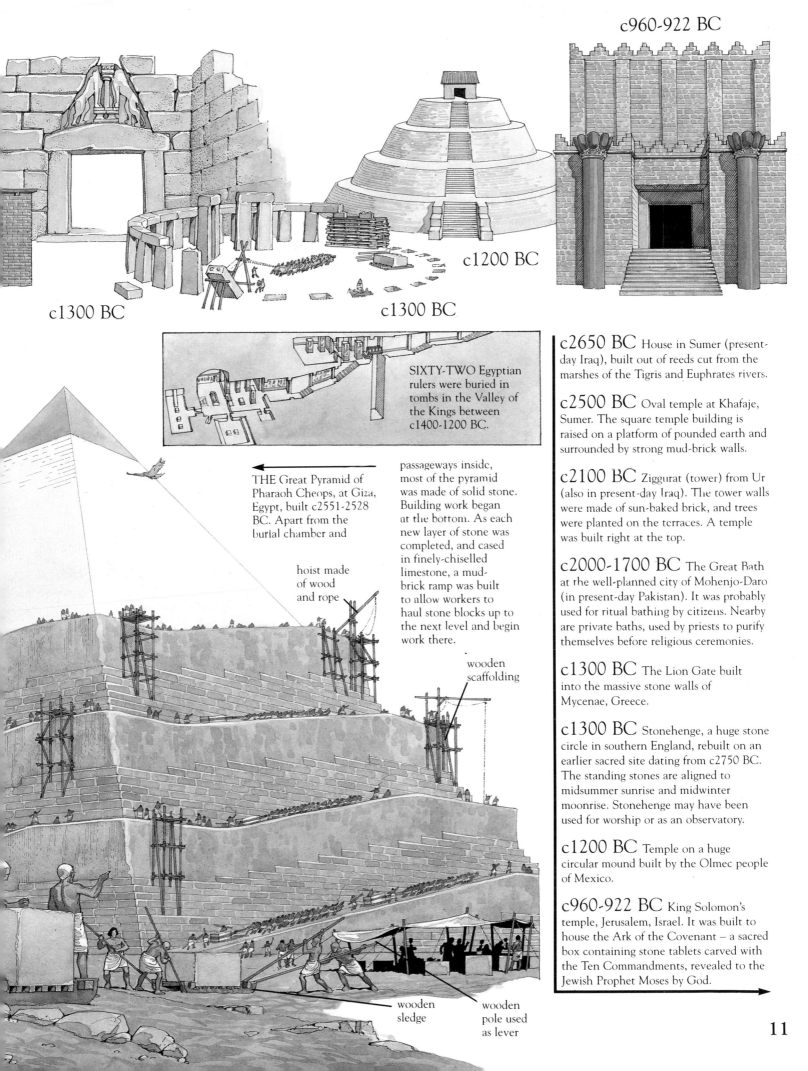

c960-922 BC

c1300 BC

c1300 BC

c1200 BC

SIXTY-TWO Egyptian rulers were buried in tombs in the Valley of the Kings between c1400-1200 BC.

THE Great Pyramid of Pharaoh Cheops, at Giza, Egypt, built c2551-2528 BC. Apart from the burial chamber and passageways inside, most of the pyramid was made of solid stone. Building work began at the bottom. As each new layer of stone was completed, and cased in finely-chiselled limestone, a mud-brick ramp was built to allow workers to haul stone blocks up to the next level and begin work there.

hoist made of wood and rope

wooden scaffolding

wooden sledge

wooden pole used as lever

c2650 BC House in Sumer (present-day Iraq), built out of reeds cut from the marshes of the Tigris and Euphrates rivers.

c2500 BC Oval temple at Khafaje, Sumer. The square temple building is raised on a platform of pounded earth and surrounded by strong mud-brick walls.

c2100 BC Ziggurat (tower) from Ur (also in present-day Iraq). The tower walls were made of sun-baked brick, and trees were planted on the terraces. A temple was built right at the top.

c2000-1700 BC The Great Bath at the well-planned city of Mohenjo-Daro (in present-day Pakistan). It was probably used for ritual bathing by citizens. Nearby are private baths, used by priests to purify themselves before religious ceremonies.

c1300 BC The Lion Gate built into the massive stone walls of Mycenae, Greece.

c1300 BC Stonehenge, a huge stone circle in southern England, rebuilt on an earlier sacred site dating from c2750 BC. The standing stones are aligned to midsummer sunrise and midwinter moonrise. Stonehenge may have been used for worship or as an observatory.

c1200 BC Temple on a huge circular mound built by the Olmec people of Mexico.

c960-922 BC King Solomon's temple, Jerusalem, Israel. It was built to house the Ark of the Covenant – a sacred box containing stone tablets carved with the Ten Commandments, revealed to the Jewish Prophet Moses by God.

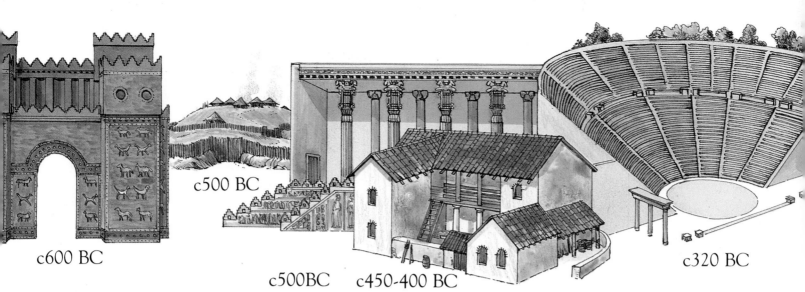

c600 BC

c500 BC

c500BC   c450-400 BC

c320 BC

THE GREEK WORLD

Kurgan (burial mound) covering the tomb of a Scythian chief, on the steppes of Central Asia, c700 BC. Tombs like these were filled with precious treasures for the chief to use in the life after death.

Through travel, trade and conquest, the Greeks came into contact with many different cultures and civilizations. Each had developed an individual style of building, which reflected not only the lives led by the people and the local building materials, but also local religious and political beliefs. For example, warlike Chinese emperors built strong walls and splendid gateways, while Indian philospher-kings beautified holy cities where religious leaders once lived.

For the Greeks, the main aim of a city was to enable men and women to live 'good' lives – to be honest, responsible citizens. They did not admire extravagance or excess. A sensible balance (the Greeks called it 'proportion') between work and pleasure, self and community, was the ideal. A city's buildings should help people live this good life. There should be decent housing, fine temples, solid government buildings, a spacious market-square, a sports hall and a theatre. And building styles, like lifestyles, should be kept in proportion. All the separate elements – doors, roofs, windows, decoration – should blend together to create a balanced whole.

THE Hanging Gardens of Babylon, built by King Nebuchanezzar around 580 BC on an artificial mountain in the centre of the city. Legends say the gardens were built to please his wife, Amytis.

THE ACROPOLIS (citadel) in Athens, Greece. Orginally a fortress, built on a high cliff, it was developed into a complex of temples and shrines during the 5th century BC, as part of government leader Pericles's scheme to rebuild and beautify the city.

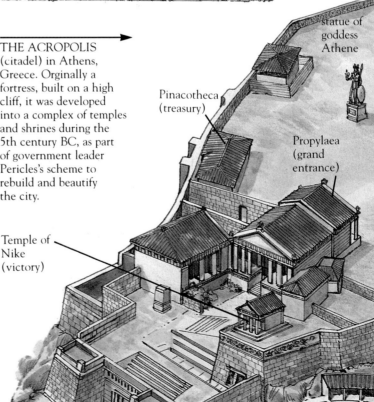

statue of goddess Athene

Pinacotheca (treasury)

Propylaea (grand entrance)

Temple of Nike (victory)

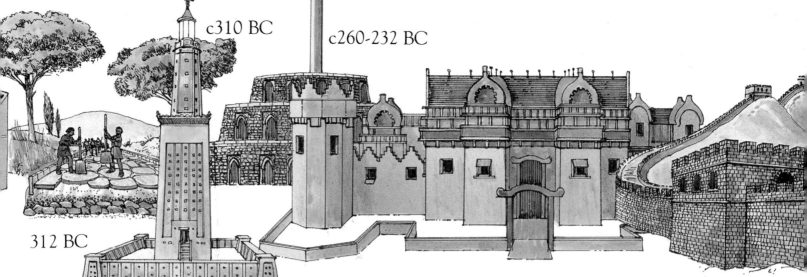

c310 BC

c260-232 BC

312 BC

c250 BC

221-207 BC

THE PARTHENON (446-431 BC), a magnificent temple dedicated to the goddess Athene, guardian of Athens, stood at the highest point of the Acropolis. It was built of sparkling white marble, and decorated with a beautiful carved frieze. It housed a statue of Athene almost 9 metres tall and decorated with gold and ivory. The Parthenon was built partly to bring prestige to the city of Athens, and partly as a memorial to Athenian soldiers who had recently been killed in wars against the Persians. Nearby were temples dedicated to Victory and to an ancient local god of snakes.

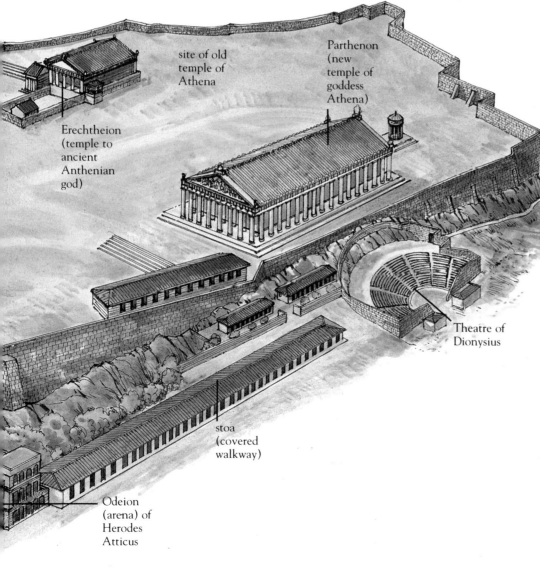

Erechtheion (temple to ancient Anthenian god)

site of old temple of Athena

Parthenon (new temple of goddess Athena)

Theatre of Dionysius

stoa (covered walkway)

Odeion (arena) of Herodes Atticus

c600 BC The Ishtar Gate, Babylon (in present-day Iraq). During the reign of King Nebuchadnezzar II (605-561 BC), strong new walls were built around the city, with splendid gates like these.

c500 BC Celtic hill-fort at Danebury, southern England. Steep earth ramparts enclose houses and granaries.

c500 BC Palace of King Darius (ruled 521-486 BC) at Persepolis (in present-day Iran).

c450-400 BC Home of a wealthy family living in Athens, the most powerful of the Greek city-states.

c320 BC Theatre at Epidaurus, Greece, designed by Polykleitos.

312 BC (begun) The Appian Way was an important Roman road. It led from the city of Rome to Brindisi, the main port for ships sailing to Greece.

c310 BC The Pharos (lighthouse) at Alexandria, in Egypt. Famous in Greek and Roman times as one of the Seven Wonders of the World.

c260-232 BC Stone pillar built by Ashoka, ruler of the Mauryan empire in India. Ashoka ordered sacred Buddhist texts and his own laws to be carved on pillars like this throughout his empire.

c250 BC City gate, Kushinagara, India, the holy city where the Buddha died.

221-207 BC During this period (the reign of Shi Huangdi, the first Chinese Emperor) the first part of the massive Great Wall of China was built.

c100 BC-AD 100

c12 BC

150 BC

c100 BC-AD 100

c10 BC-AD 100

The Roman World

Roman town house, c300-200 BC. It is built round an open courtyard, with an enclosed garden at the rear.

The Romans learned many things from the Greeks: their alphabet, their religion and their building styles. Roman temples, with their heavy pediments supported by rows of columns, follow earlier Greek designs, and Roman stonemasons copied the tools and techniques of earlier Greek builders.

By around 100 BC, people living in Rome faced three problems: getting enough fresh water, disposing of sewage and finding somewhere to live. So Roman builders dug sewers, constructed aqueducts, and designed 'insulae', the world's first blocks of flats. Roman builders discovered they could use arches to help them build high walls that would not collapse under their own weight. Tiers of arches were used to build the Colosseum – a huge arena in the heart of Rome. Roman builders also invented concrete.

By around AD 100, the Romans ruled a vast empire and Roman building styles often replaced local designs, at least for important buildings. But farmhouses worldwide continued to be built in traditional ways – local farmers knew what worked best for them.

SETTEFINESTRE (Seven Windows), a Roman villa (country house) built in Tuscany, Italy, in the 1st century AD.

top floor living rooms

INSULA (block of flats) at the port of Ostia near Rome, 1st century AD. Blocks like these were planned and built as a complete unit, often by landlords, who then let them out to rent. Shops and taverns were on the ground floor, the best apartments were on the first floor, and small, cramped, cheaper rooms were built under the roof. Communal lavatories were built in the courtyard, and there was a fountain supplying fresh water outside.

food shops

c110

c315

c80

c100

c200

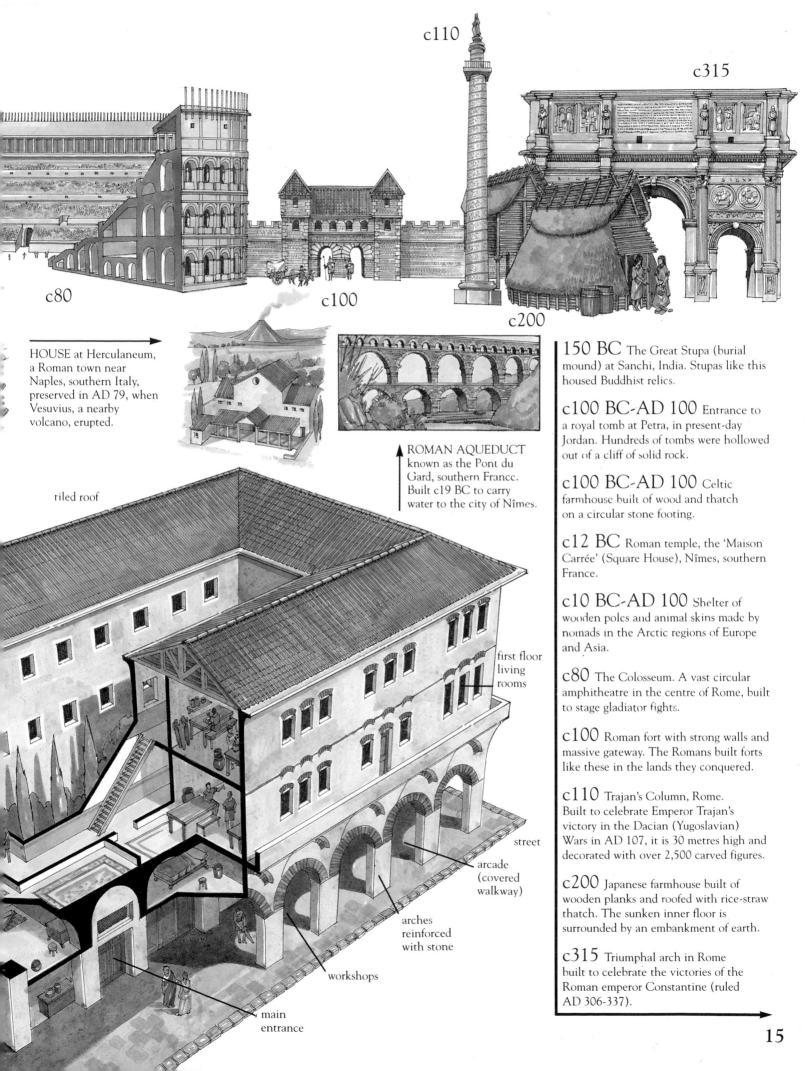

HOUSE at Herculaneum, a Roman town near Naples, southern Italy, preserved in AD 79, when Vesuvius, a nearby volcano, erupted.

ROMAN AQUEDUCT known as the Pont du Gard, southern France. Built c19 BC to carry water to the city of Nîmes.

tiled roof

first floor living rooms

street

arcade (covered walkway)

arches reinforced with stone

workshops

main entrance

150 BC The Great Stupa (burial mound) at Sanchi, India. Stupas like this housed Buddhist relics.

c100 BC-AD 100 Entrance to a royal tomb at Petra, in present-day Jordan. Hundreds of tombs were hollowed out of a cliff of solid rock.

c100 BC-AD 100 Celtic farmhouse built of wood and thatch on a circular stone footing.

c12 BC Roman temple, the 'Maison Carrée' (Square House), Nîmes, southern France.

c10 BC-AD 100 Shelter of wooden poles and animal skins made by nomads in the Arctic regions of Europe and Asia.

c80 The Colosseum. A vast circular amphitheatre in the centre of Rome, built to stage gladiator fights.

c100 Roman fort with strong walls and massive gateway. The Romans built forts like these in the lands they conquered.

c110 Trajan's Column, Rome. Built to celebrate Emperor Trajan's victory in the Dacian (Yugoslavian) Wars in AD 107, it is 30 metres high and decorated with over 2,500 carved figures.

c200 Japanese farmhouse built of wooden planks and roofed with rice-straw thatch. The sunken inner floor is surrounded by an embankment of earth.

c315 Triumphal arch in Rome built to celebrate the victories of the Roman emperor Constantine (ruled AD 306-337).

15

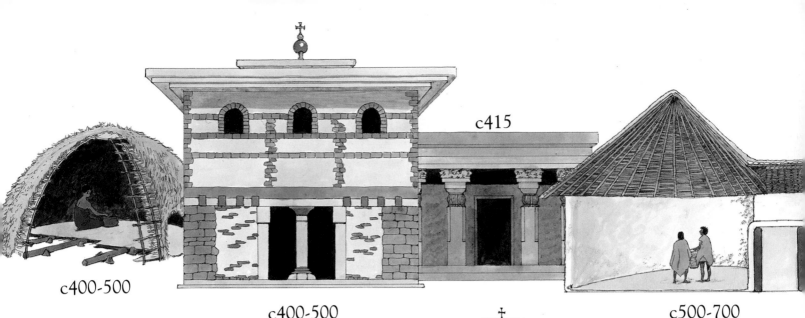

c400-500

c400-500

c415

c500-700

After Rome

The Aqueduct of Valens, Constantinople. Built between c300-400 to bring fresh water to the city.

THE BASILICA of San Vitale, Ravenna, Italy. Built during the 6th century AD and decorated with splendid mosaics.

side half-dome

buttress

The Roman empire collapsed in 476, but Roman civilization continued to flourish at the court of emperors in Constantinople (present-day Istanbul).

Constantinople had been founded by the Romans in 330, and contained many fine buildings in the Roman style: aqueducts, arenas, public monuments and strong defensive walls. But by 476 there was a difference. The emperors at Constantinople were Christian. They felt that the city needed important new buildings to proclaim their Christian faith. In 532, Emperor Justinian gave orders for a new church to be built. It was to be the largest and most splendid in Christendom. Justinian himself decided on its shape and size: it was to be roughly square and 30 metres wide. Justinian's architects were puzzled. How could anyone construct a roof that wide? No timber beams were long or strong enough. But soon they found an answer. Justinian's church would be roofed with a dome.

In other parts of the world, builders were also facing new challenges and finding new solutions. In Transvaal, the traditional wood and grass huts were coated with clay, giving them extra strength. In America, builders 'sank' homes underground, to provide shelter from the searing desert heat. In Ethiopia, builders of royal palaces could construct high walls without mortar.

BYZANTINE EMPEROR JUSTINIAN (ruled 527-565) and his wife Theodora portrayed in mosaic pictures on the walls of the Basilica of San Vitale, Ravenna (above).

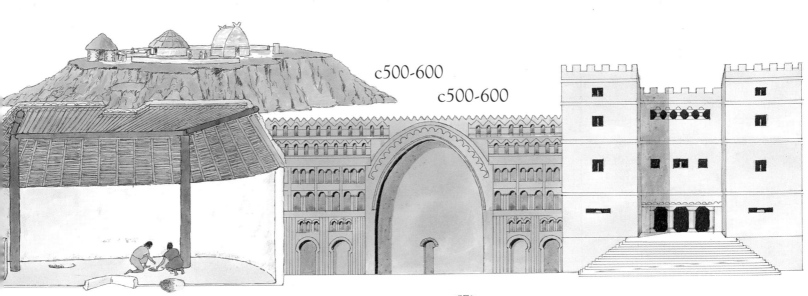

c500-600

c500-600

c600

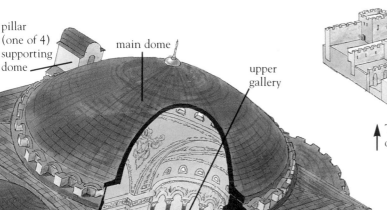

pillar (one of 4) supporting dome

main dome

upper gallery

THE TRIPLE WALLS of Constantinople, built by Emperor Constantine in the 4th century AD. The innermost wall had guardrooms and watchtowers. Outside the walls there was a deep moat.

buttress supporting wall and dome

outer wall

side aisle

SANTA SOPHIA, Constantinople, the great Christian church built on the orders of the Emperor Justinian.

c400-500 Dome-shaped hut, Transvaal, South Africa. Made of a wooden framework thatched with grass matting and plastered with clay. Inside, the walls were also coated with clay, and the floor, raised above ground level on wooden joists, was covered with thick grass mats.

c400-500 Church at Debre Damo, Ethiopia, built on a timber frame with drystone walling.

c415 Hindu temple at Sanchi, India. This shrine is a simple square room, fronted by a porch with columns topped with carved lions and bells.

c500-700 Two-roomed, sunken-pit house made by farmers from the Basketmaker Culture, New Mexico, USA. The larger room, used as living space, was lined with stone slabs. Entrance to the house was via the roof of the smaller room, which was used as a storage chamber.

c500-600 Monastery built by early Christian monks on the west coast of Ireland.

c500-600 Majestic palace gateway at Ctesiphon (in present-day Iran), capital city of the powerful Sassanian empire.

c600 Royal palace at Axum (in present-day Ethiopia). Built of stone, with walls 5 metres high, it was designed as four linked towers containing living accommodation, surrounding a central courtyard. There would have been temples and smaller government buildings nearby.

17

c600-700

794

c690

c600-800

THE END OF THE MILLENNIUM

The first mosque was the house belonging to the Prophet Muhammad (lived c570-632) in Medina, Arabia.

During the
7th to 10th centuries the faith of Islam spread from its birthplace in Arabia to North Africa, Central Asia and the Middle East. Muslim rulers also governed southern Spain. In all these countries Muslim ideas, customs and technologies mingled with older regional traditions.

Mosques, where people meet to pray and study the Qur'an (the holy book of Islam), were the most important Muslim buildings. But there were others: schools, colleges, libraries, hospitals, city gates, water fountains and tombs. Beautiful gardens were also created. Muslim architects improved earlier building techniques, creating large domed and vaulted roofs, and excelled at elaborate geometrical decorations, using ceramic tiles, mosiacs, plaster and stone.

Elsewhere, grand buildings ranged from the elegant carved and gilded wooden temples in Japan's royal capital city of Kyoto to the stone-built splendour and solidity of King Charlemagne's palace in France. For ordinary people, worldwide, homes were still roughly made of materials available nearby. Often, but not always, this was wood. In Iceland, where there are no trees, Viking builders made houses out of thick slabs of turf.

THE Dome of the Rock, Jerusalem, a mosque built in 691 on a site holy to Jews, Christians and Muslims. This building illustrates how Muslim architects improved on old building technologies, such as Byzantine domes, to create spectacular new structures.

↑ MINARET from the Great Mosque at Samarra, Iraq, built for the Caliph al-Mutawakkil in 874.

The Great Mosque in Mecca, Arabia, the holiest shrine in the Islamic world.

↑ THE Ibn Tulun mosque, in Cairo, Egypt, built during the 9th century AD.

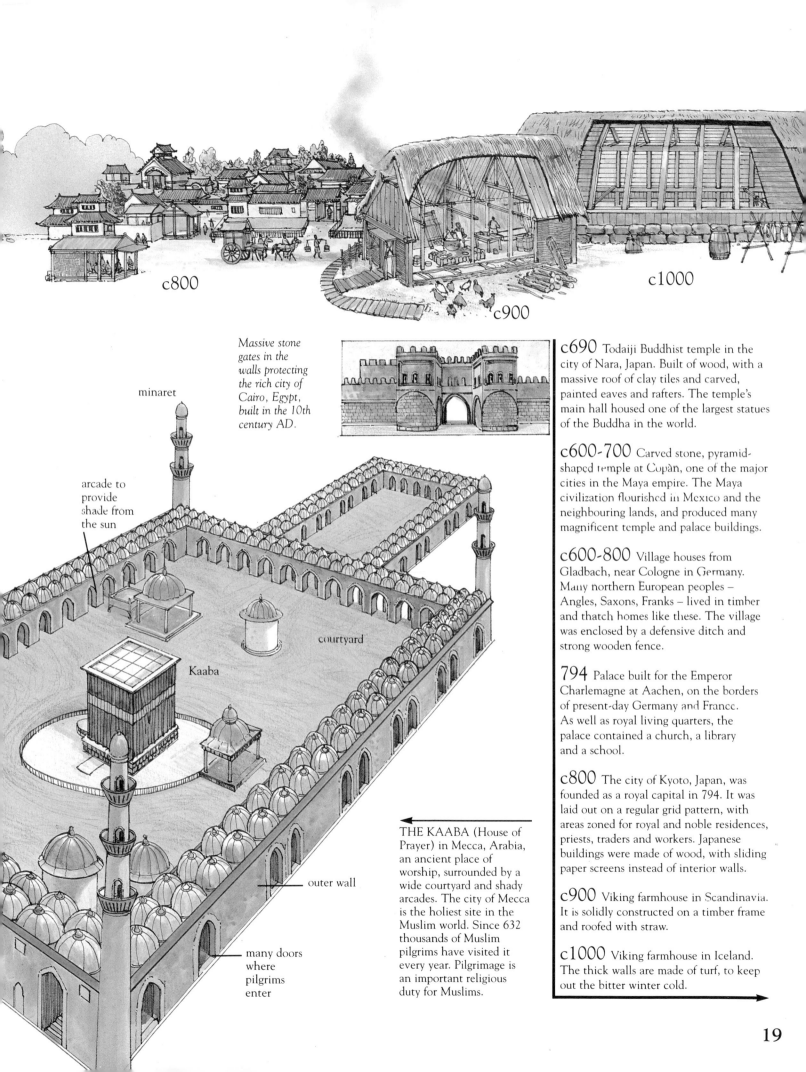

c800

c900

c1000

minaret

arcade to
provide
shade from
the sun

*Massive stone
gates in the
walls protecting
the rich city of
Cairo, Egypt,
built in the 10th
century AD.*

courtyard

Kaaba

outer wall

many doors
where
pilgrims
enter

THE KAABA (House of
Prayer) in Mecca, Arabia,
an ancient place of
worship, surrounded by a
wide courtyard and shady
arcades. The city of Mecca
is the holiest site in the
Muslim world. Since 632
thousands of Muslim
pilgrims have visited it
every year. Pilgrimage is
an important religious
duty for Muslims.

c690 Todaiji Buddhist temple in the
city of Nara, Japan. Built of wood, with a
massive roof of clay tiles and carved,
painted eaves and rafters. The temple's
main hall housed one of the largest statues
of the Buddha in the world.

c600-700 Carved stone, pyramid-
shaped temple at Copàn, one of the major
cities in the Maya empire. The Maya
civilization flourished in Mexico and the
neighbouring lands, and produced many
magnificent temple and palace buildings.

c600-800 Village houses from
Gladbach, near Cologne in Germany.
Many northern European peoples –
Angles, Saxons, Franks – lived in timber
and thatch homes like these. The village
was enclosed by a defensive ditch and
strong wooden fence.

794 Palace built for the Emperor
Charlemagne at Aachen, on the borders
of present-day Germany and France.
As well as royal living quarters, the
palace contained a church, a library
and a school.

c800 The city of Kyoto, Japan, was
founded as a royal capital in 794. It was
laid out on a regular grid pattern, with
areas zoned for royal and noble residences,
priests, traders and workers. Japanese
buildings were made of wood, with sliding
paper screens instead of interior walls.

c900 Viking farmhouse in Scandinavia.
It is solidly constructed on a timber frame
and roofed with straw.

c1000 Viking farmhouse in Iceland.
The thick walls are made of turf, to keep
out the bitter winter cold.

19

c1000

1045-1062

1063-1096

c1000

1053

THE EARLY MIDDLE AGES

Guardian statue from a temple built by the Toltec people of Mexico c1000.

PUEBLO (communal housing) c1100 at Mesa Verde, Colorado, USA. Built of stone and adobe (sunbaked clay).

TEMPLE of the Warriors, built by the Toltecs at Chichen Itza, Mexico, c1000.

By around 1000, architects and builders worldwide had perfected a great many different building techniques and styles.

Churches and cathedrals where people met to pray were built high, and tipped with turrets or spires which reached up towards the sky as if they were carrying prayers up to the heavens. Temples and shrines which housed precious holy relics were richly decorated outside with carvings (especially in India and South Asia), mosaics or real gold, emphaisizing their importance.

Secular buildings were also designed to impress. Castle builders hoped that their enemies would feel small and powerless when faced with sheer, looming walls. Japanese architects chose the shape of a phoenix when designing a new hall for the royal palace. Like the ruling dynasty, the phoenix was meant to live for ever.

However, one of the largest and most unusual buildings constructed early in the Middle Ages was probably not designed by architects or built by professional craftsmen. The village of Pueblo Bonito in America developed to meet the needs of the local people who followed a communal way of life.

central courtyard

lookout tower

roof-level walkway

strong outer wall made of sunbaked clay and stone

c1100

1194/5

1095

c1120-1150

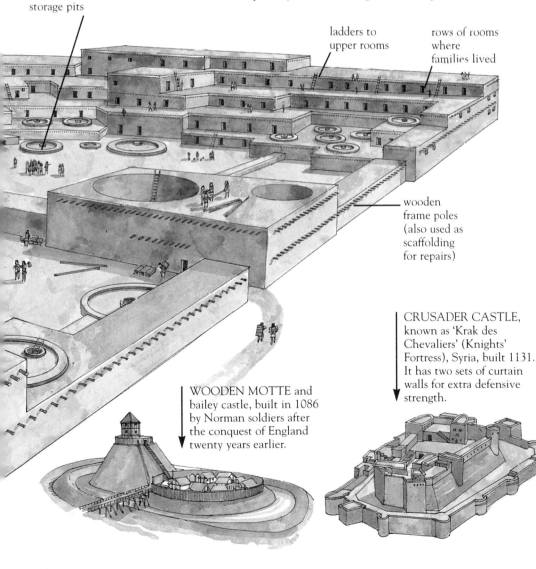

PUEBLO BONITO, NEW MEXICO, USA, dating from the 11th century, but repaired, enlarged and adapted over the next 200 years. Built by the Anasazi people using rough stone, wood and mud. Rows of sleeping accommodation, workrooms and storerooms are arranged in semicircular tiers. Access to the upper rooms is by ladder. The pueblo was deserted in the mid 14th century, possibly because a drought led to crop failure.

sunken grain storage pits

ladders to upper rooms

rows of rooms where families lived

wooden frame poles (also used as scaffolding for repairs)

WOODEN MOTTE and bailey castle, built in 1086 by Norman soldiers after the conquest of England twenty years earlier.

CRUSADER CASTLE, known as 'Krak des Chevaliers' (Knights' Fortress), Syria, built 1131. It has two sets of curtain walls for extra defensive strength.

c1000 Hindu temple at Madura, southern India. The whole building is covered with elaborate carvings, showing scenes from ancient religious myths and legends.

c1000 Traditional-style town house from Muslim Spain.

1045-1062 Church of St Sophia, Novgorod, Russia. Built in the Byzantine style, but with small windows and thick walls to suit the cold Russian weather.

1053 Buddhist temple at Uji, Japan. Named 'Phoenix Hall' because its layout looks like the bird in flight.

1063-1096 St Mark's Basilica in Venice, Italy. Built on the site of an earlier church to house relics of the saint.

1095 Monastery at Cluny, France. One of Europe's largest monasteries, with space for monks, novices, servants and guests, plus a hospital, a library and large gardens.

c1100 Canal and bridge at Suzhou, China. Part of a major engineering scheme planned by rulers of the Song dynasty.

c1120-1150 Temple and palace complex at Angkor Wat, Cambodia, built by King Suryavarman, ruler of the Khmer empire.

1194/5 Chartres cathedral, in northern France. One of the greatest buildings in the newly-fashionable Gothic style, with tall pointed windows and a soaring roof. The stained glass windows were especially fine.

1215

1215

c1250

c1200

1238-1264

Central Asian khan or caravanserai, an inn where merchants and their animals could shelter and rest, built in the 13th century.

THE HIGH MIDDLE AGES

Coral trilithon (building made of three stone pillars) from the Pacfic Ocean island of Tongatapu. Its purpose is unknown; it may have been used for observing the stars.

What are walls for? That might seem a silly question, but when we look at buildings from around 1200-1300, it is clear that not all walls were built for the same reason.

European castle walls were for defence, but even so, during the 13th century, castle designs changed. Instead of a single square keep, with massive walls a metre or more thick, castles now had several curtain walls encircling a smaller central tower. Military architects believed the curtain walls, with moats and booby-traps in between them, would make the tower harder to attack. Curtain walls were thinner than keep walls, but still needed a great deal of stone.

Traditionally, walls also supported the weight of roofs, whether on Georgian churches, Indian temples or English barns. But the walls of Europe's great Gothic cathedrals, built during the 13th century, contain very little stone and a great deal of glass. Cathedral architects had discovered how to build vaulted roofs resting on rows of pillars instead of solid walls. What had once been wall-space could now be used for windows filled with stained glass. If needed, extra support for the roof came from buttresses.

The Cathedral of Notre-Dame, Paris, France, begun around 1210. It was designed and built in typical Gothic style, with pointed arches above windows and doors. The twin towers were for bells.

c1255

1277-1307

1268

1290

SAINTE CHAPELLE, PARIS, begun c1250 as a private chapel for King Louis IX of France. The walls are almost entirely made of brilliant stained glass.

THE TRADING CITY of Novgorod, built on both banks of the River Dnieper in northern Russia, was surrounded by strong stone walls.

BEAUMARIS CASTLE, WALES. Another of Edward I's great castles (see 1277 above). It was designed with two concentric curtain walls, each fortified with towers, surrounding a central stronghold, but King Edward died in 1307 and Beaumaris was never finished.

c1200 Monastery at Mtskheta, capital city of Georgia. The church tower has been influenced by nearby Central Asian designs.

1215 Mahabodhi Buddhist temple, Pagan, Burma. Its design was based on an earlier Indian temple which housed relics of the tree under which the Buddha sat in meditation.

1215 Castle Hedingham, in eastern England. A typical square stone keep, with a turret guarding and strengthening each corner.

1238-1264 Surya Temple, Konarak, southern India. Built in the shape of the sun-god's chariot.

c1250 The Church of St George at Lalibela, in Ethiopia, carved out of solid rock.

c1255 Barn for storing wheat, Essex, eastern England. Timber-framed with brick infill and a steeply-sloping tiled roof.

1268 Kesava Hindu temple, Somnathpur, southern India. It was designed with three star-shaped sanctuaries linked to a central prayer hall. It is covered with richly detailed carvings.

1277-1307 Conwy Castle, Wales. One of eight huge fortresses built by King Edward I of England to secure his newly-conquered Welsh lands.

1290 Orvieto cathedral, in southern Italy. A fusion of older Romanesque and new Gothic styles. The front is decorated with mosaics.

c1312-1337

c1355   1370

c1300   1354

THE LATE MIDDLE AGES

Tikis, carved wooden figures believed to keep evil spirits away, protected many Maori buildings.

In almost all societies, new buildings are a sign of wealth. Europe and the Middle East had been devastated by attacks of plague in the 1340s and 1360s, but, towards the end of the century an economic recovery began, and many new buildings were designed. Often these buildings were connected with trade – town halls or guildhalls. Some, like Bruges Town Hall or the Leaning Tower of Pisa, soon became famous landmarks. Both were designed in locally-fashionable styles: Bruges' Town Hall in the newer Gothic style, Pisa's Leaning Tower in the older Romanesque.

Thousands of miles away in Africa the kings of Zimbabwe and Mali were also planning new buildings. Like European merchants, their wealth came from trade.

In contrast, royal families in Europe were rich because they owned vast amounts of land. Many commissioned new buildings in the latest designs. The hammer-beam roof of Westminster Hall was a great technical innovation because it used shorter, lighter lengths of timber, so putting less strain on walls. The pope was rich, too, but his new palace at Avignon was designed for security, not style.

MAGNIFICENT hammerbeam roof at Westminster Hall, London, c1395. A fine example of late Perpendicular building technology.

THE MARKET HALL at Bruges, in Belgium, one of the richest towns of late medieval Europe. It was designed in the latest, flamboyant Gothic style, to reflect the town's growing prosperity, and as a symbol of its power.

1370

c1380

1397

1374

c1390

A Maori 'pa' or fortress in New Zealand. Forts like these were built from around 1000-1700. Double wooden fences surround houses, food stores, lookout towers and grazing land.

THE SITE OF THE WALLED CITY of Great Zimbabwe, in southern Africa, covers over 40 hectares. Inside the strong granite walls, in parts over 10 metres high and 5 metres thick, there was a royal palace, with granaries and treasuries, a religious shrine and many small homes for servants and workers.

rooms for servants, bodyguard and officials

outer walls made of dry stone

grazing yards where cattle could be kept

c1300 The Altneuschul (Old-New Synagogue), Prague, Czech Republic. The brick gables were added soon after 1400.

c1312-1337 Sankore Mosque, Timbuktu, Africa, built for King Mansa Musa of Mali. It is made of mud-brick and rubble, coated with clay. The wooden spikes provide access for repairs.

1354 (completed) Court of the Myrtles in the Alhambra Palace, southern Spain. Built for Spain's Muslim rulers.

c1355 The bell-tower of Pisa Cathedral, Italy. Now well-known as the Leaning Tower of Pisa because its foundations have subsided, causing it to lean.

1370 Siva temple, Panataram, Java. Built as a burial place and shrine to house the ashes of Java's ruling princes.

1370 (completed) Palace of the Popes, Avignon, France. Built at a time when there were two rival popes.

1374 Church of the Transfiguration, Novgorod, Russia. Inside, the walls are decorated with wonderful frescos.

c1380 The castle as a work of art – Saumur, in France, built by the rich and cultured dukes of Berry.

c1390 Fine stone house belonging to a rich wool merchant in England.

1397 Golden Pavilion, Kyoto, Japan. A rest-house and monastery, where government leaders could go on peaceful retreat.

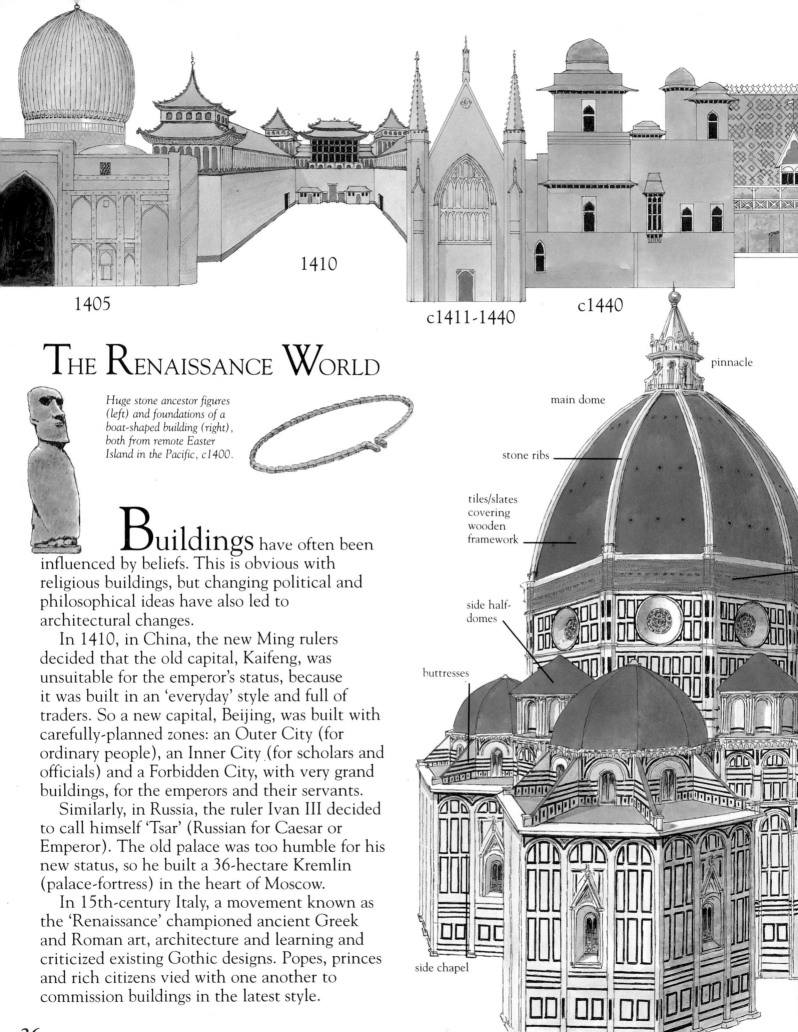

1405

1410

c1411-1440

c1440

pinnacle

main dome

stone ribs

tiles/slates
covering
wooden
framework

side half-
domes

buttresses

side chapel

THE RENAISSANCE WORLD

Huge stone ancestor figures (left) and foundations of a boat-shaped building (right), both from remote Easter Island in the Pacific, c1400.

Buildings have often been influenced by beliefs. This is obvious with religious buildings, but changing political and philosophical ideas have also led to architectural changes.

In 1410, in China, the new Ming rulers decided that the old capital, Kaifeng, was unsuitable for the emperor's status, because it was built in an 'everyday' style and full of traders. So a new capital, Beijing, was built with carefully-planned zones: an Outer City (for ordinary people), an Inner City (for scholars and officials) and a Forbidden City, with very grand buildings, for the emperors and their servants.

Similarly, in Russia, the ruler Ivan III decided to call himself 'Tsar' (Russian for Caesar or Emperor). The old palace was too humble for his new status, so he built a 36-hectare Kremlin (palace-fortress) in the heart of Moscow.

In 15th-century Italy, a movement known as the 'Renaissance' championed ancient Greek and Roman art, architecture and learning and criticized existing Gothic designs. Popes, princes and rich citizens vied with one another to commission buildings in the latest style.

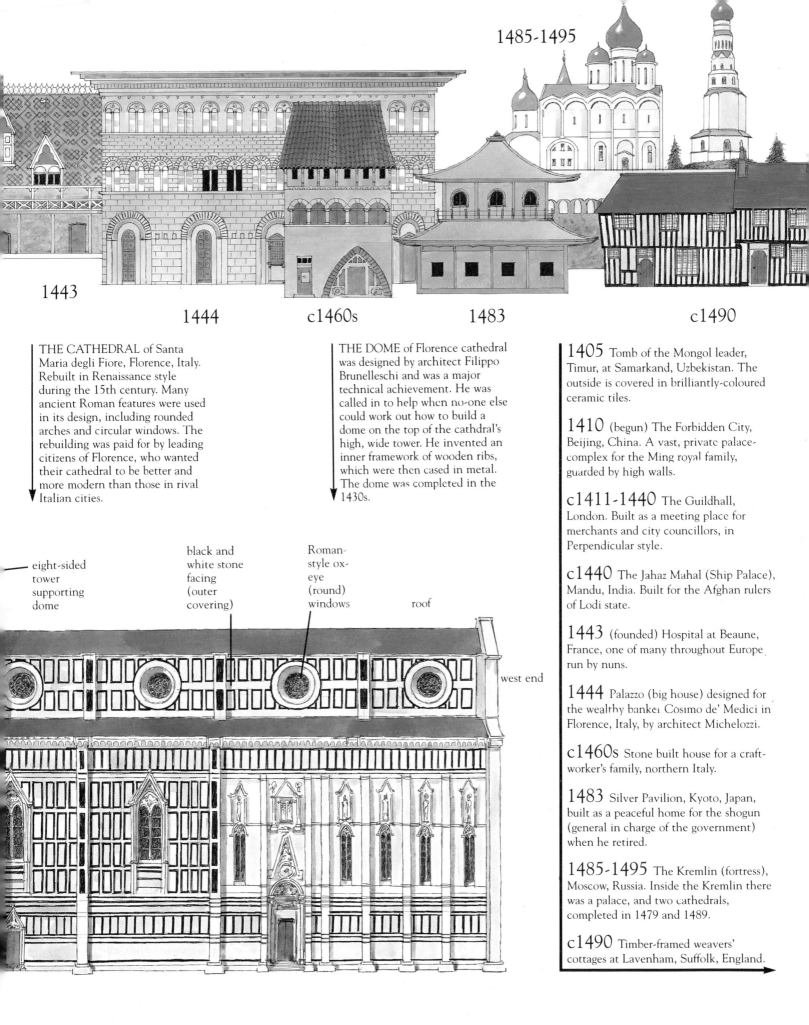

1485-1495

1443

1444

c1460s

1483

c1490

THE CATHEDRAL of Santa Maria degli Fiore, Florence, Italy. Rebuilt in Renaissance style during the 15th century. Many ancient Roman features were used in its design, including rounded arches and circular windows. The rebuilding was paid for by leading citizens of Florence, who wanted their cathedral to be better and more modern than those in rival Italian cities.

THE DOME of Florence cathedral was designed by architect Filippo Brunelleschi and was a major technical achievement. He was called in to help when no-one else could work out how to build a dome on the top of the cathdral's high, wide tower. He invented an inner framework of wooden ribs, which were then cased in metal. The dome was completed in the 1430s.

1405 Tomb of the Mongol leader, Timur, at Samarkand, Uzbekistan. The outside is covered in brilliantly-coloured ceramic tiles.

1410 (begun) The Forbidden City, Beijing, China. A vast, private palace-complex for the Ming royal family, guarded by high walls.

c1411-1440 The Guildhall, London. Built as a meeting place for merchants and city councillors, in Perpendicular style.

c1440 The Jahaz Mahal (Ship Palace), Mandu, India. Built for the Afghan rulers of Lodi state.

1443 (founded) Hospital at Beaune, France, one of many throughout Europe run by nuns.

1444 Palazzo (big house) designed for the wealthy banker Cosimo de' Medici in Florence, Italy, by architect Michelozzi.

c1460s Stone built house for a craft-worker's family, northern Italy.

1483 Silver Pavilion, Kyoto, Japan, built as a peaceful home for the shogun (general in charge of the government) when he retired.

1485-1495 The Kremlin (fortress), Moscow, Russia. Inside the Kremlin there was a palace, and two cathedrals, completed in 1479 and 1489.

c1490 Timber-framed weavers' cottages at Lavenham, Suffolk, England.

eight-sided tower supporting dome

black and white stone facing (outer covering)

Roman-style ox-eye (round) windows

roof

west end

27

1515-1520   1546   1554-1560   c1560s   1565   1568

THE 16TH CENTURY

Tenochtitlán, the capital of the Aztec empire.

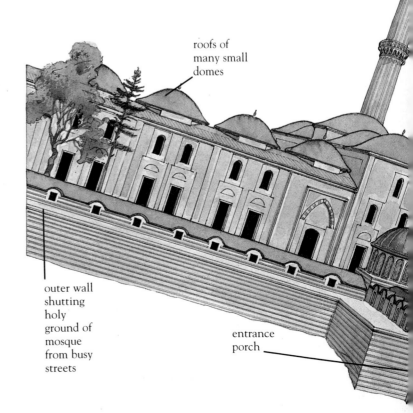

THE Château (grand country house) of Chambord, France, completed 1547. It was designed for King François I by the Italian architect Domenico da Cortona who used a mixture of Italian Renaissance and traditional French features.

By 1500,

Renaissance fashions in buildings had spread from Italy to the rest of Europe. A typical Renaissance building had design features 'borrowed' from Greek and Roman temples and monuments: columns, pediments and rounded arches. In northern Europe, these Renaissance features were combined with local materials to create regional styles. English Renaissance buildings, for example, were usually built of red brick, not white marble as in Italy or Greece.

The 16th century was also a time of exploration. Spanish adventurers, like Cortés, brought back descriptions of amazing buildings in the American 'New World'. The Aztecs' capital, Tenochtitlán, he reported, rivalled any city in Europe. Cortés destroyed Tenochtitlán in 1521. In India, Vijayanagar, another great city full of wonderful buildings, was devastated by Mughal invaders.

In Turkey and the Middle East, the Muslim Ottoman empire was fast becoming a world power. During the reign of Sultan Suleyman the Magnificent (1520-1566) some of the largest and most beautiful mosques in the world were built.

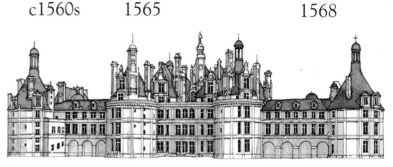

roofs of many small domes

outer wall shutting holy ground of mosque from busy streets

entrance porch

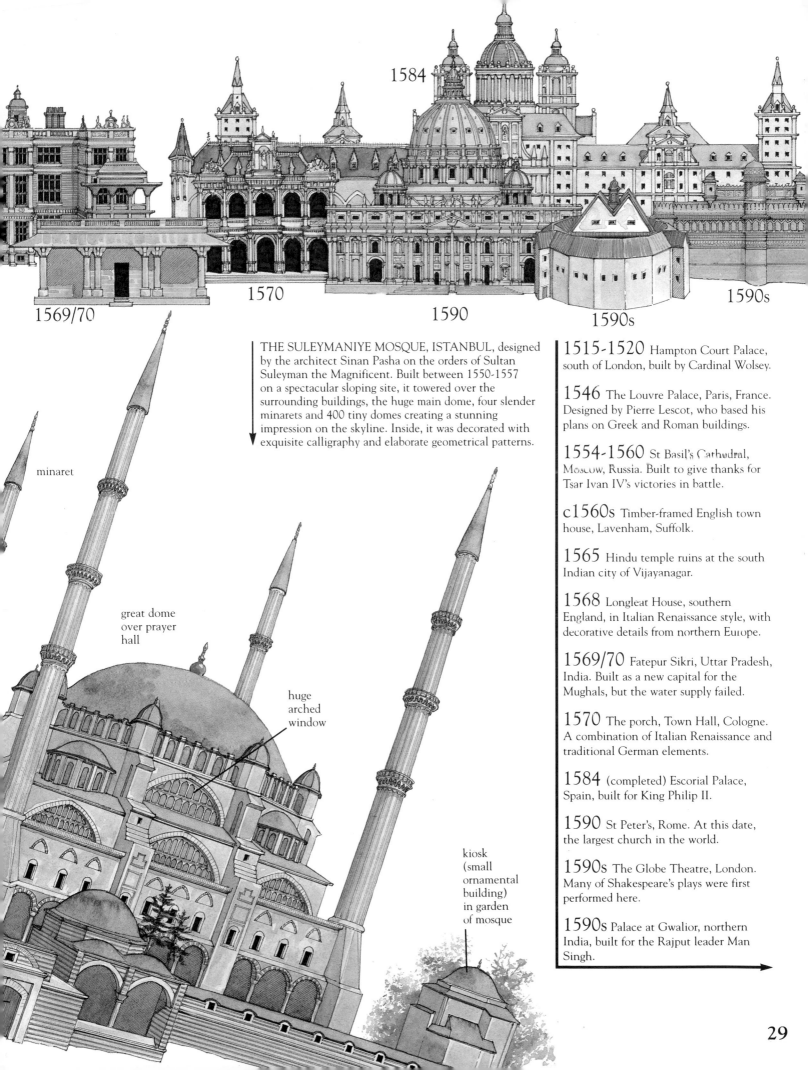

1584

1570

1569/70

1590

1590s

1590s

minaret

great dome over prayer hall

huge arched window

kiosk (small ornamental building) in garden of mosque

THE SULEYMANIYE MOSQUE, ISTANBUL, designed by the architect Sinan Pasha on the orders of Sultan Suleyman the Magnificent. Built between 1550-1557 on a spectacular sloping site, it towered over the surrounding buildings, the huge main dome, four slender minarets and 400 tiny domes creating a stunning impression on the skyline. Inside, it was decorated with exquisite calligraphy and elaborate geometrical patterns.

1515-1520 Hampton Court Palace, south of London, built by Cardinal Wolsey.

1546 The Louvre Palace, Paris, France. Designed by Pierre Lescot, who based his plans on Greek and Roman buildings.

1554-1560 St Basil's Cathedral, Moscow, Russia. Built to give thanks for Tsar Ivan IV's victories in battle.

c1560s Timber-framed English town house, Lavenham, Suffolk.

1565 Hindu temple ruins at the south Indian city of Vijayanagar.

1568 Longleat House, southern England, in Italian Renaissance style, with decorative details from northern Europe.

1569/70 Fatepur Sikri, Uttar Pradesh, India. Built as a new capital for the Mughals, but the water supply failed.

1570 The porch, Town Hall, Cologne. A combination of Italian Renaissance and traditional German elements.

1584 (completed) Escorial Palace, Spain, built for King Philip II.

1590 St Peter's, Rome. At this date, the largest church in the world.

1590s The Globe Theatre, London. Many of Shakespeare's plays were first performed here.

1590s Palace at Gwalior, northern India, built for the Rajput leader Man Singh.

1619-1622

c1640

1608

1622

1628

THE 17TH CENTURY

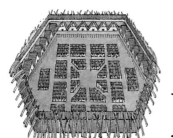

Fort built by French colonial settlers in Quebec, Canada, c1630. It was surrounded by a wooden stockade to protect it from attack by Native Americans.

In the early part of the century, Renaissance designs were still very popular in Europe, especially for high-status buildings, like the Banqueting Hall, London, commissioned by King Charles I of England. But traditional building styles and materials were coming back into fashion, especially in Dutch and English towns. Dutch town houses were built several storeys high, to make maximum use of scarce building space. Most had storage lofts in the roofs, which were typically decorated with 'curly' gable ends.

Traditional, 'vernacular' building styles – that is, homes of the type lived in by ordinary people – were taken across the Atlantic by English and French settlers to the new colonies in America.

Towards the end of the century in Europe Renaissance styles of architecture were replaced by a new architectural fashion, the Baroque. It was based on, and developed from, Renaissance-style Greek and Roman designs, but used them in a freer, more dramatic way. Simple forms, like columns or domes, were twisted or elongated to create striking shapes. The palace of Versailles, France, is a fine example of the Baroque style.

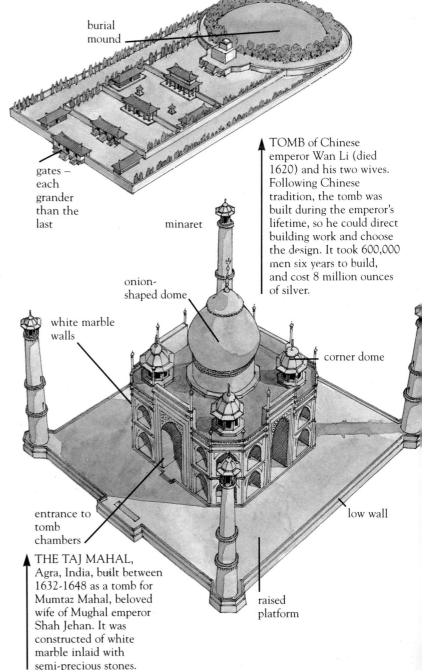

burial mound

gates – each grander than the last

minaret

TOMB of Chinese emperor Wan Li (died 1620) and his two wives. Following Chinese tradition, the tomb was built during the emperor's lifetime, so he could direct building work and choose the design. It took 600,000 men six years to build, and cost 8 million ounces of silver.

onion-shaped dome

white marble walls

corner dome

entrance to tomb chambers

low wall

THE TAJ MAHAL, Agra, India, built between 1632-1648 as a tomb for Mumtaz Mahal, beloved wife of Mughal emperor Shah Jehan. It was constructed of white marble inlaid with semi-precious stones.

raised platform

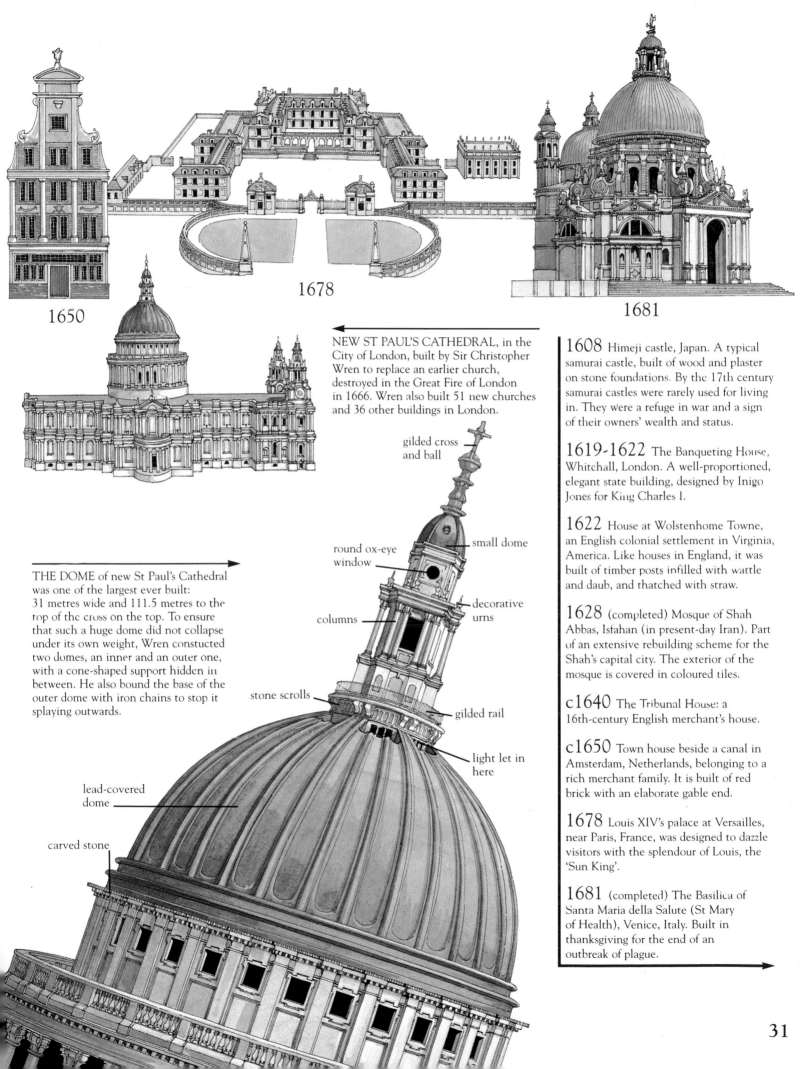

1650

1678

1681

NEW ST PAUL'S CATHEDRAL, in the City of London, built by Sir Christopher Wren to replace an earlier church, destroyed in the Great Fire of London in 1666. Wren also built 51 new churches and 36 other buildings in London.

gilded cross and ball

round ox-eye window

small dome

columns

decorative urns

stone scrolls

gilded rail

light let in here

THE DOME of new St Paul's Cathedral was one of the largest ever built: 31 metres wide and 111.5 metres to the top of the cross on the top. To ensure that such a huge dome did not collapse under its own weight, Wren constucted two domes, an inner and an outer one, with a cone-shaped support hidden in between. He also bound the base of the outer dome with iron chains to stop it splaying outwards.

lead-covered dome

carved stone

1608 Himeji castle, Japan. A typical samurai castle, built of wood and plaster on stone foundations. By the 17th century samurai castles were rarely used for living in. They were a refuge in war and a sign of their owners' wealth and status.

1619-1622 The Banqueting House, Whitchall, London. A well-proportioned, elegant state building, designed by Inigo Jones for King Charles I.

1622 House at Wolstenhome Towne, an English colonial settlement in Virginia, America. Like houses in England, it was built of timber posts infilled with wattle and daub, and thatched with straw.

1628 (completed) Mosque of Shah Abbas, Isfahan (in present-day Iran). Part of an extensive rebuilding scheme for the Shah's capital city. The exterior of the mosque is covered in coloured tiles.

c1640 The Tribunal House: a 16th-century English merchant's house.

c1650 Town house beside a canal in Amsterdam, Netherlands, belonging to a rich merchant family. It is built of red brick with an elaborate gable end.

1678 Louis XIV's palace at Versailles, near Paris, France, was designed to dazzle visitors with the splendour of Louis, the 'Sun King'.

1681 (completed) The Basilica of Santa Maria della Salute (St Mary of Health), Venice, Italy. Built in thanksgiving for the end of an outbreak of plague.

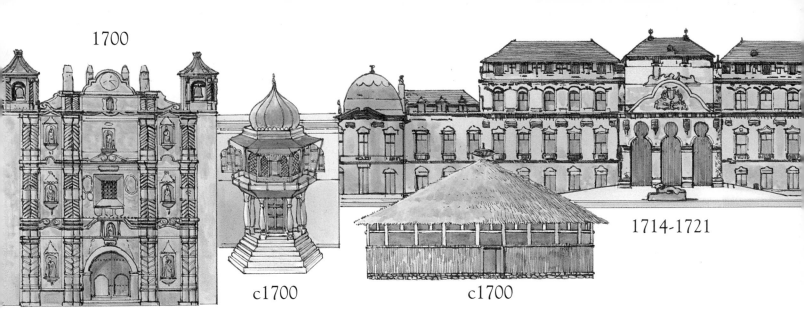

1700

c1700

c1700

1714-1721

THE 18TH CENTURY

American colonial farmhouse, New England, c1700. Built on a timber frame and clad with wooden planks and shingles.

In the 18th century a remarkable range of buildings was under construction worldwide, from wood-and-plaster Chinese temples and circular churches made of reeds to the world's first structure built of cast iron. In Europe, the Baroque style still remained popular. Churches and monasteries, some very old, were torn down and rebuilt in elaborate Baroque designs. Baroque was also fashionable for the interiors of royal palaces. Favourite colour schemes were white and gold.

The most advanced European buildings were now influenced by technological innovations. Often, these were due to experience gained in war or, like the rebuilt Eddystone lighthouse off the south-west coast of England, were to meet commercial transport needs. Military architects like Vauban planned French new towns, as well as army forts.

One of the most ambitious building schemes was organized by Tsar Peter the Great of Russia. He ordered a whole new city, St Petersburg, to be built on marshy land bordering the icy Baltic Sea. So many of the construction workers died that the city was said to be 'built on bones'.

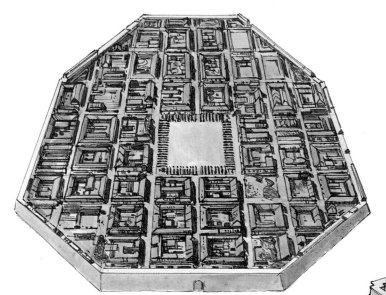

NEW TOWN AT NEUF-BRISACH, northern France, built 1699-1712. Designed by Vauban on a rectangular grid and surrounded by strong walls. Inside, there is a church, a public square, civic buildings and a barracks, as well as houses and apartment blocks.

THE WINTER PALACE, St Petersburg, Russia. Built by Tsar Peter the Great as part of his mammouth project to establish a whole new city on the banks of the Neva River. The palace was enlarged to its present size during the reign of Peter's daughter, Empress Elizabeth (1741-62).

portico (stone porch with columns, in ancient Greek style)

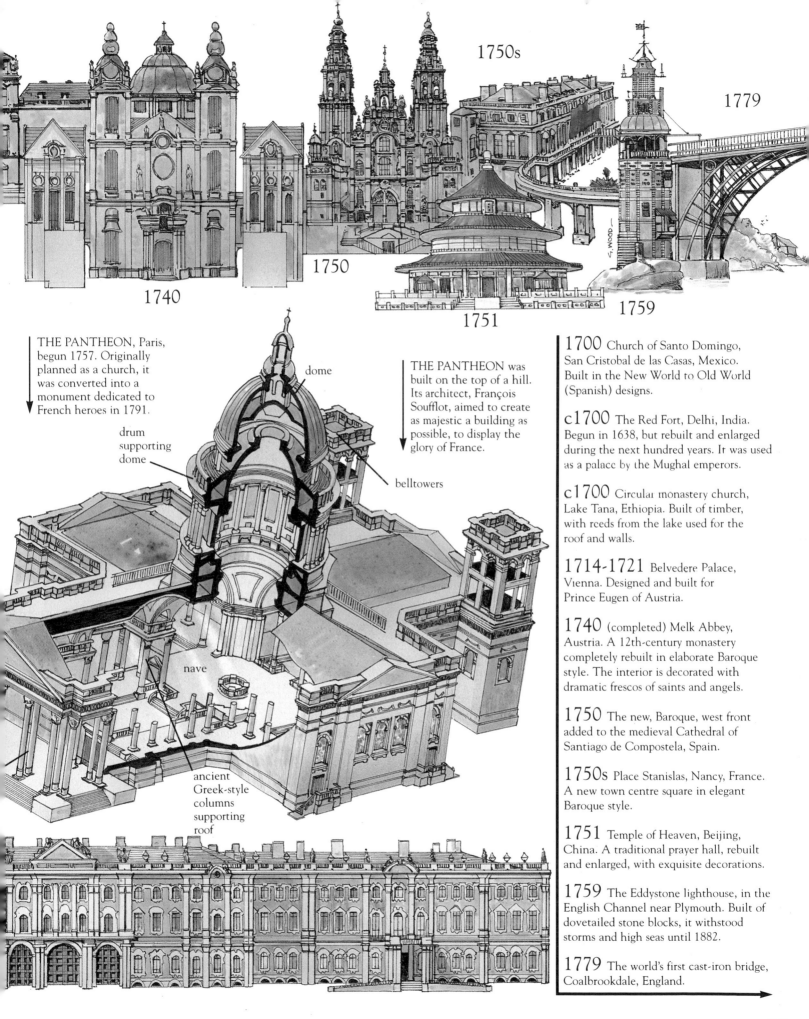

1750s

1779

1740

1750

1751

1759

THE PANTHEON, Paris, begun 1757. Originally planned as a church, it was converted into a monument dedicated to French heroes in 1791.

dome

drum supporting dome

THE PANTHEON was built on the top of a hill. Its architect, François Soufflot, aimed to create as majestic a building as possible, to display the glory of France.

belltowers

nave

ancient Greek-style columns supporting roof

1700 Church of Santo Domingo, San Cristobal de las Casas, Mexico. Built in the New World to Old World (Spanish) designs.

c1700 The Red Fort, Delhi, India. Begun in 1638, but rebuilt and enlarged during the next hundred years. It was used as a palace by the Mughal emperors.

c1700 Circular monastery church, Lake Tana, Ethiopia. Built of timber, with reeds from the lake used for the roof and walls.

1714-1721 Belvedere Palace, Vienna. Designed and built for Prince Eugen of Austria.

1740 (completed) Melk Abbey, Austria. A 12th-century monastery completely rebuilt in elaborate Baroque style. The interior is decorated with dramatic frescos of saints and angels.

1750 The new, Baroque, west front added to the medieval Cathedral of Santiago de Compostela, Spain.

1750s Place Stanislas, Nancy, France. A new town centre square in elegant Baroque style.

1751 Temple of Heaven, Beijing, China. A traditional prayer hall, rebuilt and enlarged, with exquisite decorations.

1759 The Eddystone lighthouse, in the English Channel near Plymouth. Built of dovetailed stone blocks, it withstood storms and high seas until 1882.

1779 The world's first cast-iron bridge, Coalbrookdale, England.

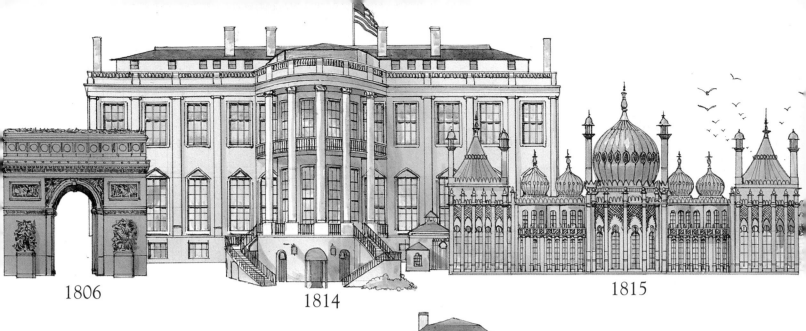

1806
1814
1815

The Early 19th Century

Cramped, insanitary back-to-back houses were built by factory-owners in British industrial cities to provide cheap housing for low-paid workers.

THE LARGEST
19th-century terraced houses could be five or six storeys high, and have twenty rooms. Some were for entertaining, some were for family use and others were for servants.

stairs

QUARRY BANK MILL, Styal, in north-west England. Originally built in 1783, but doubled in size, as shown here, in 1801. It contained machines to spin cotton thread.

The Industrial Revolution changed the world. It changed the world's buildings, too. In Europe and North America the new mills and factories were larger than almost all previous buildings and were designed to suit machines not people. Before drawing up their plans, architects and builders studied all the stages of an industrial process, such as spinning cotton or smelting iron, and designed the building around them.

Conditions inside early factories were hot, noisy, dirty and dangerous. The factory workers' living conditions were little better. Their new homes, built next to the factories, were cramped and polluted.

Most Far Eastern, African and Asian countries were not industrialized until the 20th century. In the early 19th century, ordinary people still lived and worked in traditional ways.

Old-style buildings remained popular in Europe and America. Old designs gave instant respectability. That is why Napoleon ordered a monument (the Arc de Triomphe in Paris) copying ancient Roman designs. He wanted to appear like a hero of old.

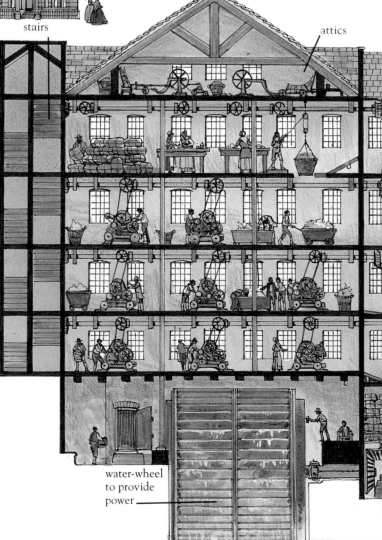

attics

water-wheel to provide power

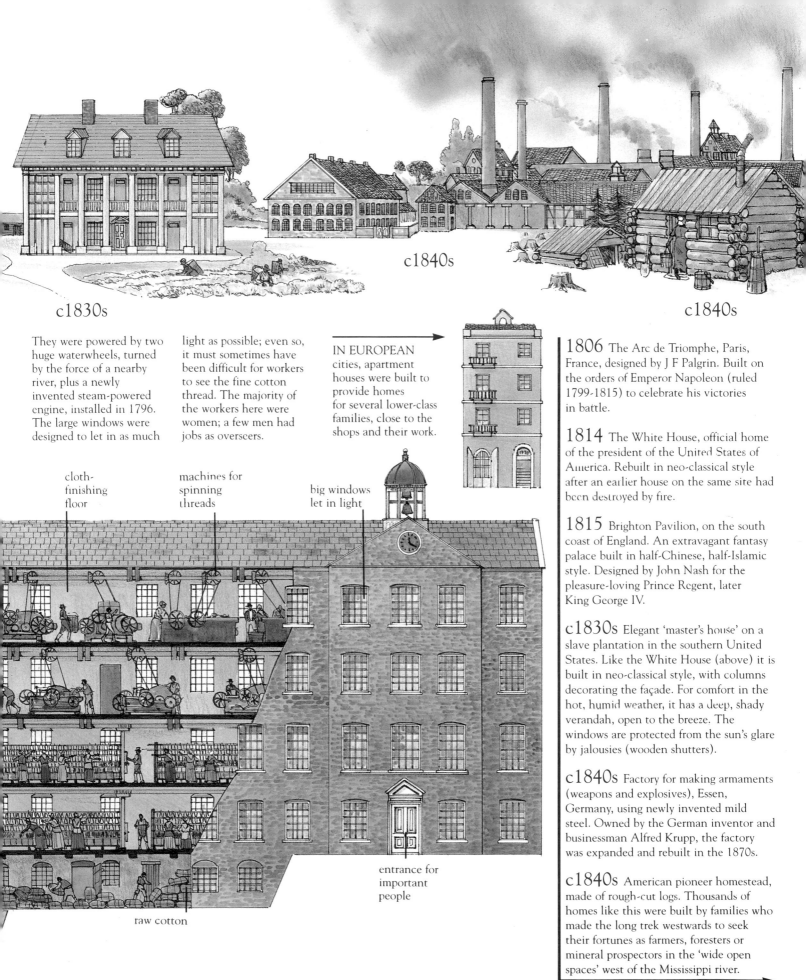

c1840s

c1830s

c1840s

They were powered by two huge waterwheels, turned by the force of a nearby river, plus a newly invented steam-powered engine, installed in 1796. The large windows were designed to let in as much light as possible; even so, it must sometimes have been difficult for workers to see the fine cotton thread. The majority of the workers here were women; a few men had jobs as overseers.

IN EUROPEAN cities, apartment houses were built to provide homes for several lower-class families, close to the shops and their work.

cloth-finishing floor

machines for spinning threads

big windows let in light

entrance for important people

raw cotton

1806 The Arc de Triomphe, Paris, France, designed by J F Palgrin. Built on the orders of Emperor Napoleon (ruled 1799-1815) to celebrate his victories in battle.

1814 The White House, official home of the president of the United States of America. Rebuilt in neo-classical style after an earlier house on the same site had been destroyed by fire.

1815 Brighton Pavilion, on the south coast of England. An extravagant fantasy palace built in half-Chinese, half-Islamic style. Designed by John Nash for the pleasure-loving Prince Regent, later King George IV.

c1830s Elegant 'master's house' on a slave plantation in the southern United States. Like the White House (above) it is built in neo-classical style, with columns decorating the façade. For comfort in the hot, humid weather, it has a deep, shady verandah, open to the breeze. The windows are protected from the sun's glare by jalousies (wooden shutters).

c1840s Factory for making armaments (weapons and explosives), Essen, Germany, using newly invented mild steel. Owned by the German inventor and businessman Alfred Krupp, the factory was expanded and rebuilt in the 1870s.

c1840s American pioneer homestead, made of rough-cut logs. Thousands of homes like this were built by families who made the long trek westwards to seek their fortunes as farmers, foresters or mineral prospectors in the 'wide open spaces' west of the Mississippi river.

1851

1851-1863

1864

1861-1874

THE LATE 19TH CENTURY

St Pancras Station and Hotel, London. Designed by Gilbert Scott in the Gothic style, it was built in the 1860s.

The Industrial Revolution generated many new building materials, especially iron and glass. Mass production made them cheap and plentiful, and the new railways could transport them long distances with ease. Iron and glass also opened up new possibilities for imaginative designers. Iron was strong and rigid, and could be cast or wrought (bent) into a variety of exciting shapes. Although glass was fragile, it was bright and transparent. Now builders could construct offices, flats, stations and department stores in new ways.

Iron girders could also replace the timber frames traditionally used for houses. A 'box' of girders, riveted together, formed a secure skeleton ready to be cased in glass, brick or concrete. Buildings like this could be taller and wider than ever before. 'Skyscrapers' (high towers of offices or flats) originated in this way.

Many people were enthusiastic about the new building technology – but not everyone. In Europe and America a few architects called for a return to traditional construction methods. Other critics disliked the 'factory-made' look. They campaigned for a 'Gothic revival', romantically harking back to an imaginary past.

THE SUEZ CANAL linked the Mediterranean with the Red Sea. It was designed by French engineers, is 160 kilometres long and took 10 years to build. It opened in 1869.

The clocktower of the Houses of Parliament, London. Designed in Gothic Revival (mock medieval) style by Sir Charles Barry and Augustus Pugin and completed in 1860.

steep, slate-covered roof

Gothic-style pointed windows

carved stone decoration

Big Ben clock face

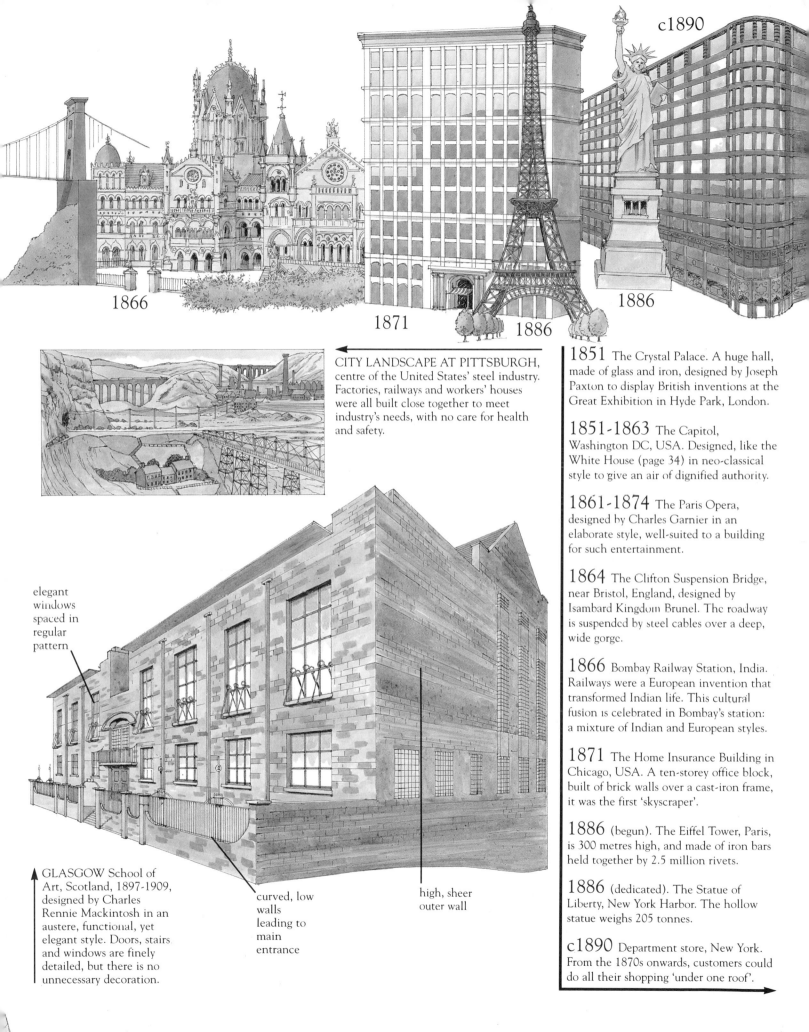

1866

1871

1886

1886

c1890

CITY LANDSCAPE AT PITTSBURGH, centre of the United States' steel industry. Factories, railways and workers' houses were all built close together to meet industry's needs, with no care for health and safety.

elegant windows spaced in regular pattern

GLASGOW School of Art, Scotland, 1897-1909, designed by Charles Rennie Mackintosh in an austere, functional, yet elegant style. Doors, stairs and windows are finely detailed, but there is no unnecessary decoration.

curved, low walls leading to main entrance

high, sheer outer wall

1851 The Crystal Palace. A huge hall, made of glass and iron, designed by Joseph Paxton to display British inventions at the Great Exhibition in Hyde Park, London.

1851-1863 The Capitol, Washington DC, USA. Designed, like the White House (page 34) in neo-classical style to give an air of dignified authority.

1861-1874 The Paris Opera, designed by Charles Garnier in an elaborate style, well-suited to a building for such entertainment.

1864 The Clifton Suspension Bridge, near Bristol, England, designed by Isambard Kingdom Brunel. The roadway is suspended by steel cables over a deep, wide gorge.

1866 Bombay Railway Station, India. Railways were a European invention that transformed Indian life. This cultural fusion is celebrated in Bombay's station: a mixture of Indian and European styles.

1871 The Home Insurance Building in Chicago, USA. A ten-storey office block, built of brick walls over a cast-iron frame, it was the first 'skyscraper'.

1886 (begun). The Eiffel Tower, Paris, is 300 metres high, and made of iron bars held together by 2.5 million rivets.

1886 (dedicated). The Statue of Liberty, New York Harbor. The hollow statue weighs 205 tonnes.

c1890 Department store, New York. From the 1870s onwards, customers could do all their shopping 'under one roof'.

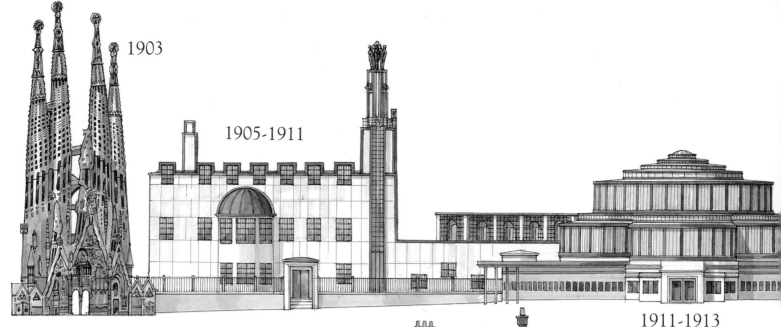

1903

1905-1911

1911-1913

THE EARLY 20TH CENTURY

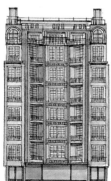

Apartment house designed by Auguste Perret, Paris, 1902-1903.

Around 1900, industrial technology combined with new ideas of what was beautiful to create a revolutionary modern style. It originated in Europe and America, but later spread to many parts of the world.

What made a building modern? Partly materials: glass, concrete and metal. Partly appearance: early 20th century buildings aimed at pure, clean lines, with no unnecessary decoration. Most important of all, 'form followed function'. Every inch was carefully planned, to create a sense of uncluttered spaciousness and to promote efficiency.

Some people admired the modern style's simplicity; others found it cold and unfriendly. During the 1920s and 1930s, mock-Tudor houses proved popular with British purchasers, though they were despised by serious architects. Other building styles, like Art Deco, introduced more colour and fun. New scientific discoveries also influenced buildings – wrought iron for fireproof stairs meant that buildings could be taller; research stations, factories and even cinemas were built in futuristic shapes.

HOMES in the garden city of Letchworth, south-east England, based on Ebenezer Howard's pioneering town plans published in *Garden Cities of Tomorrow*, 1913.

MOCK-TUDOR HOUSE in Chiselhurst, Kent, c1920. Comfortable, but backward-looking houses like this were built in the English 'home counties' during the 1920s and 1930s.

The Schroder-Schrader house, Utrecht, Netherlands, built 1924. Designed by the avant-garde architect Gerrit Rietveld, along pure, clean, simple lines.

APARTMENTS at Brüchfeldstrasse, Frankfurt, Germany, 1925. Designed by Ernst May. The whole street is planned as a single structure, made up of identical repeated 'units'.

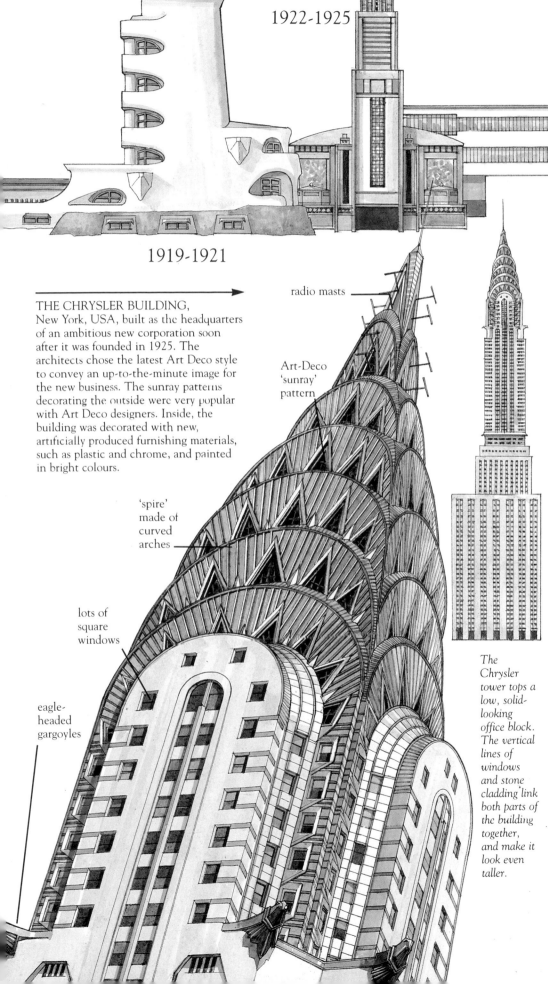

1922-1925

1919-1921

radio masts

THE CHRYSLER BUILDING,
New York, USA, built as the headquarters
of an ambitious new corporation soon
after it was founded in 1925. The
architects chose the latest Art Deco style
to convey an up-to-the-minute image for
the new business. The sunray patterns
decorating the outside were very popular
with Art Deco designers. Inside, the
building was decorated with new,
artificially produced furnishing materials,
such as plastic and chrome, and painted
in bright colours.

Art-Deco
'sunray'
pattern

'spire'
made of
curved
arches

lots of
square
windows

eagle-
headed
gargoyles

1925

*The
Chrysler
tower tops a
low, solid-
looking
office block.
The vertical
lines of
windows
and stone
cladding link
both parts of
the building
together,
and make it
look even
taller.*

1903 Church of the Sagrada Familia
(Holy Family), Barcelona, Spain. This was
originally planned as a conventional neo-
gothic building, but in 1903 architect
Antoni Gaudí began to add fantastic
towers and turrets to the roof, and
decorated them with free-style mosaics of
colourful broken tiles. The result is unlike
anything built before – or since.

1905-1911 Palais Stocklet, Brussels,
Belgium. A luxurious private house in Art
Nouveau style designed by Josef
Hoffmann, using costly materials
including marble and bronze.

1911-1913 Centennial Hall, Breslau
(present-day Wrocław), Poland. Designed
by Max Berg to house an important
exhibition. Built of reinforced concrete,
the dome covers an area of 5,300 square
metres and is 42 metres high.

1919-1921 Einstein Tower,
Potsdam, Germany. Designed by Erich
Mendelsohn as a scientific observatory for
use by the great physicist Albert Einstein.
In this building, Mendelsohn combined
flowing, 'organic' shapes copied from
nature with futuristic technology.

1922-1925 Church of Notre-Dame,
Le Raincy, near Paris, France, designed
by Auguste Perret. A traditional church
building, but made in modern materials,
reinforced and pre-cast concrete, instead
of stone.

1925 The Bauhaus, Dessau, Germany.
The most important design college in
Europe, where avant-garde artists and
architects were trained. Designed by
Walter Gropius, the college principal, in
'constructivist' style.

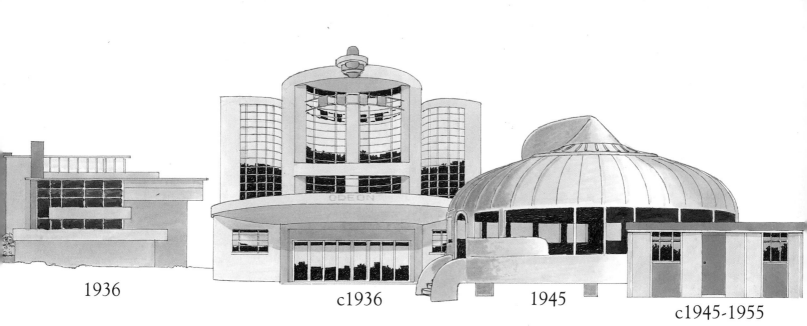

1936

c1936

1945

c1945-1955

THE MID 20TH CENTURY

Chemical factory, Nottinghamshire, England. Steel-framed concrete and glass were used for many 1930s factory buildings.

↑ CORRIDOR at the Johnson Wax Building, Wisconsin, USA, 1936-39. The interior is lit with 33 kilometres of flourescent tubes.

brightly-painted balconies

E arly 20th-century buildings, in the 'modern' style, were simple, quiet and stylish. But to some people they were also very boring. What was wrong with enormous size, exaggerated curves, fantastic skylines or science-fiction shapes? New methods of construction using sheet metal and reinforced concrete meant that a building could be moulded to almost any shape an architect liked. The examples on these pages show some of the designs this spirit of experimentation produced.

Mid-20th-century buildings were influenced by technology in another way. Architects like the American, Buckminster Fuller, experimented with the idea of buildings made by machine. Factories could either make complete houses, ready to be delivered, or else they could make prefabricated parts, which could easily be joined together to create an almost instant home.

Not every architect was swept along by these ideas. The German designer, Mies van der Rohe, continued to create monumental buildings of pure, elegant form. His achievements still influence many architects today.

UNITE d'Habitation, Marseilles, France. An enormous block of flats, designed by architect Le Corbusier, who called it 'a machine for living' and built 1947-1952. It contains 337 duplex (two-storey) flats, arranged on fourteen floors. Each has a balcony, to catch the southern sun. Inside, each floor is arranged around a wide, central corridor, which Le Corbusier described as an 'internal street'.

pylons (legs) raise the block off the ground

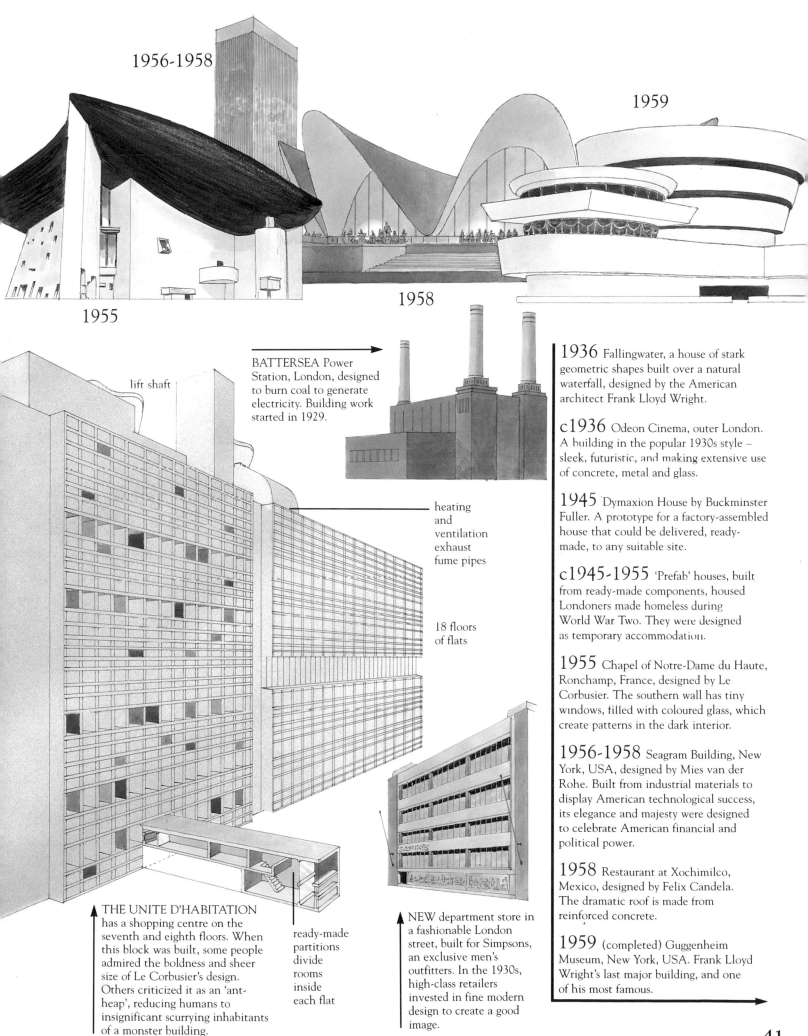

1956-1958

1959

1955

1958

lift shaft

BATTERSEA Power Station, London, designed to burn coal to generate electricity. Building work started in 1929.

heating and ventilation exhaust fume pipes

18 floors of flats

THE UNITE D'HABITATION has a shopping centre on the seventh and eighth floors. When this block was built, some people admired the boldness and sheer size of Le Corbusier's design. Others criticized it as an 'ant-heap', reducing humans to insignificant scurrying inhabitants of a monster building.

ready-made partitions divide rooms inside each flat

NEW department store in a fashionable London street, built for Simpsons, an exclusive men's outfitters. In the 1930s, high-class retailers invested in fine modern design to create a good image.

1936 Fallingwater, a house of stark geometric shapes built over a natural waterfall, designed by the American architect Frank Lloyd Wright.

c1936 Odeon Cinema, outer London. A building in the popular 1930s style – sleek, futuristic, and making extensive use of concrete, metal and glass.

1945 Dymaxion House by Buckminster Fuller. A prototype for a factory-assembled house that could be delivered, ready-made, to any suitable site.

c1945-1955 'Prefab' houses, built from ready-made components, housed Londoners made homeless during World War Two. They were designed as temporary accommodation.

1955 Chapel of Notre-Dame du Haute, Ronchamp, France, designed by Le Corbusier. The southern wall has tiny windows, filled with coloured glass, which create patterns in the dark interior.

1956-1958 Seagram Building, New York, USA, designed by Mies van der Rohe. Built from industrial materials to display American technological success, its elegance and majesty were designed to celebrate American financial and political power.

1958 Restaurant at Xochimilco, Mexico, designed by Felix Candela. The dramatic roof is made from reinforced concrete.

1959 (completed) Guggenheim Museum, New York, USA. Frank Lloyd Wright's last major building, and one of his most famous.

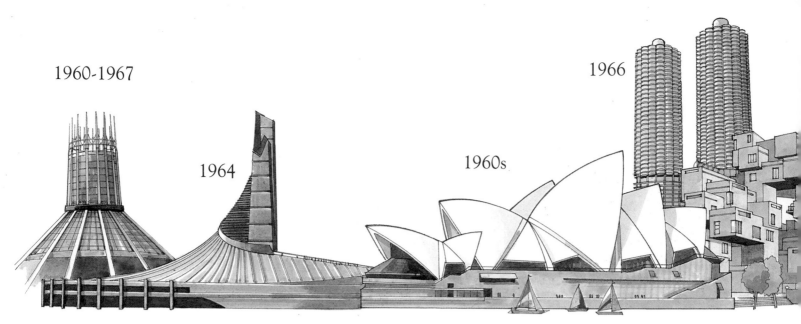

1960-1967

1964

1960s

1966

THE 1960s TO THE PRESENT

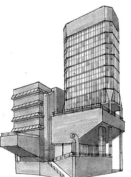

Engineering laboratory, University of Leicester, England. Designed by James Stirling and James Gowan, 1959-1963, using industrial materials and construction techniques, such as metallised glass and industrial brick.

In 1992
HRH the Prince of Wales launched a scathing attack on modern British architecture. He criticized the buildings for being brutally ugly, for being out of keeping with their surroundings and for their massive scale. Many people have since supported the Prince's views.

But others find late 20th-century buildings bold and exciting. They admire the technology that enables architects to create huge, airy structures out of shimmering glass. They admire the patterns made by criss-cross steel struts and are amused by buildings with their drainpipes on the outside.

Post-Modern buildings, like the A T & T skyscraper in New York which has an 18th-century decoration on top, may seem jokey, but they are more serious than that. Post-Modern architects argue that buildings can look like whatever we choose, regardless of past fashions or rules. Only then will they really be fit for peoples' needs. These theories have influenced some of the very latest buildings – high-tech tents, based on shelters first constructed around 30,000 years ago.

THE POMPIDOU CENTRE, PARIS, France. A large arts complex, designed by Richard Rogers and Enzo Piano and completed in 1976. It attracted both praise and criticism for its use of industrial building methods, such as panels of glass suspended from a tubular steel frame. Traditionally, a building's essential services (water, power, drains) are hidden away. Here they are a feature, with brightly coloured pipes winding round the outside of the building, almost like decoration.

ventilation ducts

walls of glass

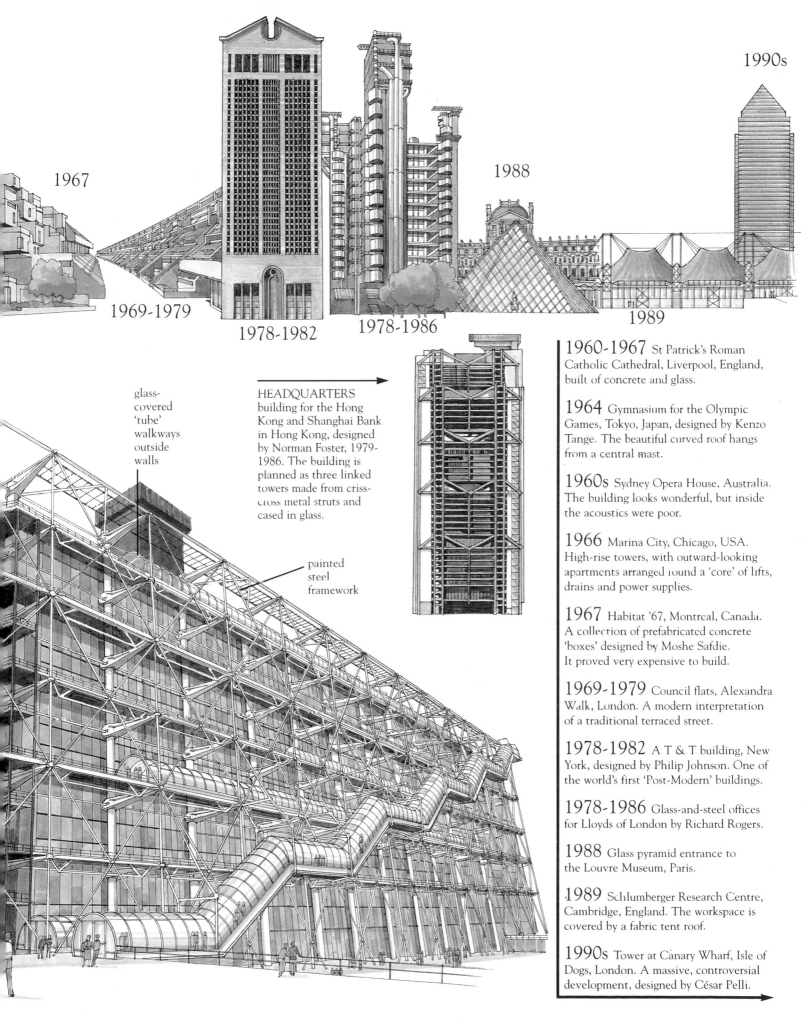

1967

1969-1979

1978-1982

1988

1978-1986

1989

1990s

glass-covered 'tube' walkways outside walls

HEADQUARTERS building for the Hong Kong and Shanghai Bank in Hong Kong, designed by Norman Foster, 1979-1986. The building is planned as three linked towers made from criss-cross metal struts and cased in glass.

painted steel framework

1960-1967 St Patrick's Roman Catholic Cathedral, Liverpool, England, built of concrete and glass.

1964 Gymnasium for the Olympic Games, Tokyo, Japan, designed by Kenzo Tange. The beautiful curved roof hangs from a central mast.

1960s Sydney Opera House, Australia. The building looks wonderful, but inside the acoustics were poor.

1966 Marina City, Chicago, USA. High-rise towers, with outward-looking apartments arranged round a 'core' of lifts, drains and power supplies.

1967 Habitat '67, Montreal, Canada. A collection of prefabricated concrete 'boxes' designed by Moshe Safdie. It proved very expensive to build.

1969-1979 Council flats, Alexandra Walk, London. A modern interpretation of a traditional terraced street.

1978-1982 A T & T building, New York, designed by Philip Johnson. One of the world's first 'Post-Modern' buildings.

1978-1986 Glass-and-steel offices for Lloyds of London by Richard Rogers.

1988 Glass pyramid entrance to the Louvre Museum, Paris.

1989 Schlumberger Research Centre, Cambridge, England. The workspace is covered by a fabric tent roof.

1990s Tower at Canary Wharf, Isle of Dogs, London. A massive, controversial development, designed by César Pelli.

43

Building Facts

Egyptian pharaoh Akenhaten (ruled 1370-1353 BC) founded a whole new city on the west bank of the River Nile, and dedicated it to the god of the Sun Disk. But pharaohs who ruled after him thought that Akenhaten's beliefs were wrong, and so the whole city was destroyed.

Geomancy is an ancient, traditional Chinese belief about the best place to site a building. Ideally, according to this belief, a new building should have a road to the west, mountains to the north, still water to the south and running water to the east.

Today, many people admire the pure white marble of ancient Greek temples. They might be surprised to learn that these temples – like the carvings that decorated them – were originally brightly painted, and decorated with metal ornaments and gold leaf.

The ancient Greek theatre at Epidaurus, built in the 4th century BC, could seat an audience of 14,000 people. The Colosseum in Rome (see page 14) could seat 70,000.

The Romans built the world's first shopping mall. It was called Trajan's Market, in Rome, and was built during the 2nd century AD. It housed about 150 businesses and shops.

The Romans employed specially trained sailors to handle the massive canvas sheets that they used as a temporary roof covering the vast arena of the Colosseum, built around AD 80. Nobody else had the necessary expertise. Sometimes they covered the floor with more large canvas sheets, flooded the arena and staged mock sea-battles.

The oldest wooden building in the world is a Buddhist temple at Horyuji, Japan. It was built around AD 670.

The 12th-century temple complex at Angkor Wat in Cambodia (modern Kampuchea) is one of the biggest buildings in Asia. Its central tower is 64 metres high and its base measures 183 x 213 metres.

Over 20,000 captives were sacrificed to the gods when a new temple was dedicated in the Aztec capital city of Tenochtitlán in 1487.

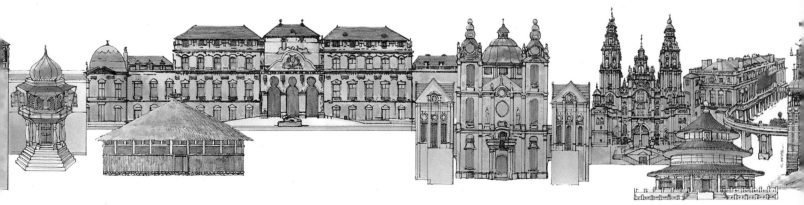

SOME IMPORTANT ARCHITECTS BORN BEFORE 1900

c2600 BC Imhotep, ancient Eyptian architect. According to Egyptian chroniclers he designed the great Step Pyramid at Saqqara, and was the first person to build in stone.

c500-c400 BC Phidias, ancient Greek sculptor and architect. He designed the Parthenon, the great temple to Athene, in Athens.

c100 BC Vitruvius, Roman architect and writer. His books on building design inspired architects and, centuries later, influenced architects of the Italian Renaissance.

1377-1456 Filippo Brunelleschi, Italian architect, one of the pioneers of the Renaissance style.

1452-1519 Leonardo da Vinci, Italian artist, scientist and inventor. His ideas influenced many other Italian architects at the time.

1475-1564 Michelangelo Buonarotti, Italian sculptor, painter and architect. His most famous works include the Farnese Palace, Rome, and the decorations for the Sistine Chapel, also in Rome.

1632-1723 Sir Christopher Wren, British architect. Famous for plans to rebuild the City of London after the Great Fire in 1666.

1728-1792 Robert Adam, British architect and interior decorator, famous for his neo-classical designs.

1809-1891 Baron Georges Haussmann, French architect who redesigned the layout of Paris.

1868-1928 Charles Rennie Mackintosh, Scottish artist and architect, who worked in Art-Nouveau style.

1869-1959 Frank Lloyd Wright, American architect, who experimented with industrial materials and dramatic modern designs.

1885-1965 Le Corbusier (Charles Edouard Jeanneret), French architect who pioneered massive communal buildings, and experimented with free-flowing forms.

1886-1969 Ludwig Mies van der Rohe, German architect, pioneer of stark, simple, uncluttered modern design.

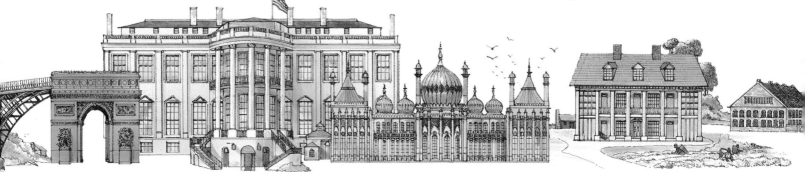

GLOSSARY

Acropolis The highest, safest place in a Greek city, where temples and other important buildings were sited. The best known is the Acropolis in Athens on which the Parthenon is built.

Arch A structure made up of wedge-shaped stones, carefully fitted together, resting on pillars at either side. The weight of the stones pressing downwards holds the arch together.

Art Deco A style of art and architecture popular in the late 1920s and 1930s. It featured sharp, angular patterns, bright colours and abstract (non-realistic) designs. Art Deco buildings often made use of 'new' materials, such as steel, plastic and glass.

Art Nouveau A style of art and architecture popular around 1900, featuring tall, thin structures, elegant lines and sweeping curves. Flowers, waves and women with extravagantly long hair were often used as decoration in Art Nouveau designs.

Back-to-back Houses joined together at the back wall – each faces in the opposite direction to the other. Back-to-back houses have no gardens and no through ventilation.

Baroque A style of architecture popular from around 1650-1750, featuring vast, elaborate twists and curves and dramatic decoration.

Buttress A wall built up against another building (usually at right angles) to support it and stop it falling outwards.

Byzantine A rich, bold, elaborate style of architecture and decoration originating in the city of Byzantium (later Constantinople, now Istanbul), in around 300-900. It was based on Roman designs.

Cast iron Iron that is heated until it melts, then poured into moulds. It can support very heavy weights, but is rather brittle.

Constructivist A style of architecture which emphasizes the way a building has been designed and constructed.

Dome A rounded structure – shaped like half a sphere – used as a roof. Putting a large round dome on a square building posed problems for Byzantine and Muslim architects. They solved these problems by designing pendentives – curved triangular sections of stonework or brickwork which carried the weight of the dome down on to strong pillars below.

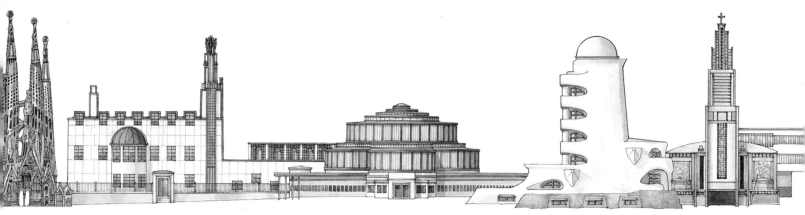

Gable The triangular top section of a wall under a sloping roof.

Gothic A style of architecture popular in around 1200-1350, featuring tall, pointed arches and high vaulted roofs.

Gothic revival A style of decoration and architecture popular in the 19th century. It copied medieval Gothic designs.

Home Counties The counties (Kent, Surrey, Hertfordshire, Essex, Middlesex) bordering London, capital city of the UK.

Infill Building material (usually brick or wattle and daub) used to fill the spaces between upright posts in a timber frame.

Longhouse A building with living space for people at one end, and stabling for animals at the other.

Mild steel A strong, lightweight, very tough form of iron.

Mock Tudor A style popular in the 19th and early 20th centuries, which copied English 16th-century timber-framed building styles.

Neo-classical Later copy of classical (that is, ancient Greek and Roman) style.

Neo-Gothic Later copy of Gothic style.

Pediment Triangular-shaped gable. Important part of Greek and Roman buildings, often decorated with sculpture.

Perpendicular Building style popular c1350-1450, with high roofs, tall columns, high, flat-topped arches, straight lines and simple decoration.

Post-Modern A style popular since the 1970s. It experiments with shapes and patterns borrowed from many periods and mixes them with modern technology to create quirky, individual designs.

Renaissance An artistic and philosophical movement inspired by the ideas, arts and achievements of ancient Greece and Rome. Very important as an influence on building styles in Europe during the 15th and 16th centuries.

Romanseque A style of building popular in Europe from c1000-1200, featuring rounded arches, low, barrel-shaped roofs and massive rounded columns.

Wattle and daub Twigs (wattle) and clay or mud (daub) mixed together and used to fill in the spaces between wooden uprights in a timber-framed building.

INDEX

Page numbers in bold refer to captions.

A

Acropolis **12**, **13**
adobe 20
Africa **8**, 17, 18, 24, 25, **25**, 34
Alhambra Palace 25
America 16, 30, 31, **32**, 34, 35, 36, 38, 41; *see also* USA
Angkor Wat 21
aqueducts 14, **15**, 16, **16**
Arc de Triomphe 34, 35
arches 14, **27**, 28, **39**
Art Deco 38, 39
Art Nouveau 39
Athens **12**, **13**
Aztecs 28, **28**

B

Babylon **12**, 13
barns 22, 23
Baroque style 30, 32, 33
Beijing 26, 27, 33
bricks 8, **9**, 11, **11**, 25, 28, 31, 36, 37, **42**
bridges 21, 33, 37
Brighton Pavilion 35
Bruges Town Hall 24, **24**
Brunelleschi, Filippo **27**
Buddha/Buddhism 13, 15, 19, 21, 23
buttresses 22, **26**

C

Capitol, the 37
Çatal Hüyük **9**
cast iron 32, 33, 36, 37
castles 20, **21**, 22, 23, **23**, 25, 31
cathedrals 20, 21, 22, **22**, 27, **27**, **31**, 33, 43
Central Asia **12**, 18, **22**, 23
Cheops, Great Pyramid of **11**
China 9, 12, 13, 21, 26, 27, **30**, 33, 35
  Great Wall of 13
Chrysler Building, the **39**

churches 16, 17, 19, 20, 21, 22, 23, **23**, 25, 29, 31, 32, **32**, 33, **33**, 39, 41
cinemas 38, 41
Coalbrookdale 33
Colosseum, the 14, 15
columns 15, 17, 28, 30, **31**, **32**, **33**, 35
concrete 14, 36, 38, 39, 40, **40**, 41, 43
Constantinople 16, **16**, **17**
Corbusier, Le **40**, 41, **41**
Crystal Palace, the 37
curtain walls **21**, 22, **23**

D, E, F

department stores 36, 37, **37**
domes 16, 18, **18**, **26**, 27, 29, 30, **30**, 31, **33**, 39

Egypt 10, **10**, 11, 12, **18**, 19
Eiffel Tower 37
England 11, 13, 23, 25, 27, 29, 30, 31, 33, **34**, 35, 37, **38**, 43, **43**
Ethiopia 16, 17, 23, 33

factories 34, 35, **37**, 38, 40
factory-built houses 40, 41
Falling Water 41
farmhouses 9, 14, 15, 19, **32**
flats 14, **14**, 36, **40**, 43
Florence 27, **27**
forts/fortresses **25**, 26, 27, 32, 33
France **15**, 18, 19, 21, **22**, 25, 27, **28**, 29, 30, 31, 32, **33**, 34, 35, **40**, 41
Fuller, Buckminster 40, 41

G, I

gardens **12**, 18, 21
Germany 19, 29, 35, **38**, 39
glass 22, 36, **36**, 37, 38, **40**, **40**, 41, **42**, 43, **43**
Gothic style 21, 22, **22**, 23, 24, 26
'Gothic Revival' 36, **36**
granaries 13, **25**
Greece/Greeks 11, 12, 13, 14, 26, 28, 29, 30

India 12, 13, 15, 17, 20, 21, 23, 27, 28, 29, **30**, 33, 37
Industrial Revolution, the 34, 36
Iran 13, 17, 31
Iraq 11, 13, 18
iron 36, **36**, 37
Istanbul 16, 29
Italy **14**, **15**, **16**, 21, 23, 25, 26, 27, **27**, 28, 31

J, K, L

Japan 15, 18, 19, 20, 21, 25, 27, 31, 43
Jerusalem 11, **18**

Kremlin, the 26, 27
Kyoto 18, 19, 25, 27

Lepenski Vir 9
lighthouses 13, 32, 33
London **24**, 27, 29, 30, 31, 36, 37, 41, **41**, 43
longhouses 9
Louvre Palace 29, 43

M

Mackintosh, Charles Rennie **37**
Mali 24, 25
Maya 19
Mexico 11, 19, **20**, 33, 41
Middle East 18, 24, 28
military monuments **13**, **15**, **33**, 34, 35
mills 34, **34**, **35**
Mohenjo-daro 11
monasteries 21, 23, 25, 32, 33
Moscow 26, 27
mosques 18, **18**, 25, 28, 29, **29**, **30**, 31
mud 8, **9**, 21
mud bricks 11, **11**, 25
Mughals 28, 29, 33
Mycenae 11

N, O

Napoleon, Emperor 34, 35
neo-classical 35, 37
neo-gothic 39
Netherlands 9, 31, **38**

New Mexico 17, **21**
new towns 32, **32**, 38
New York 37, **39**, 41, 42, 43

offices 36, 37, **39**, 43
Olmecs 11

P

palaces 8, 10, 13, 16, 17, 18, 19, 20, 21, 24, **25**, 27, 29, 30, **32**, 32, 33
Pantheon, the **33**
Paris **22**, 23, 29, 31, **33**, 34, 37, 38, 39, **42**, 43
Parthenon, the **13**
Paxton, Joseph 37
Perpendicular style **24**, 27
Persepolis 13
Peter the Great 32, **32**
Petra 15
Pisa, Leaning Tower of 24, **25**
Post-Modern 42, 43
'prefabs' 41
pueblos 20, **20**
pyramids 10, **10**, 11, 43

R

railways 36, **36**, 37, **37**
Renaissance, the 26, **27**, 28, **28**, 29, 30
Rohe, Mies van der 40, 41
Romanesque style 23, 24
Rome/Romans 13, 14, **14**, 15, **15**, 16, 26, **27**, 28, 29, 30, 34
roofs 8, 12, 16, 17, 18, 21, 22, 24, **24**, **27**, 30, **36**, 43
Russia 9, 21, **23**, 25, 26, 27

S

shops **14**, 35
shrines **12**, 17, 20, 25
Sinan Pasha **29**
skyscrapers 36, 37, 42
Spain 18, 21, 25, 29, 33, 39
St Petersburg 32, 32
stained glass 21, 22, **23**
Statue of Liberty 37
steel 35, **37**, 37, 42, 43
stone 9, 10, **11**, 17, 18, 20, **21**, 33

Stonehenge 11
Suleyman the Magnificent 28

T

Taj Mahal **30**
temples 8, 9, 10, 11, **11**, 12, **12**, 14, 15, 17, 18, 19, **20**, 20, 21, 22, 23, 28, 29, 32, 33
Tenochtitlán 28, **28**
tents 9, 42, 43
thatch 8, 15, 17, 19, 30
theatres 12, 13, 29
tiles 19, 23, **26**, 27, **38**, 39
Toltecs **20**
tombs 10, **10**, **12**, 15, 27, **30**
townhouses **14**, 21, 29, 30, 31
turf walls 9, 18
Turkey **9**, 28

U, V

Ur 11
USA 35, 37, **37**, **39**, **40**, 41, 43

vaulting 18
Venice 21, 31
Versailles 30, 31
Vijayanagar 28, 29
Vikings 18, 19
villas, Roman **14**

W, Z

walls 8, 9, 14, 16, 17, 19, 22, **23**, 24, 27, 37
  city 13, **22**, 25, 32
  defensive 12, 16, **17**, 21, 22, 27
water supplies 14, **14**, **15**, 16, 29, 34
wattle and daub 9, 31
White House, the 35
windows 12, 22, **22**, 27, 31, 35, **36**, 39
Wren, Sir Christopher **31**
Wright, Frank Lloyd 41
wrought iron 36, 38

Zimbabwe 24, **25**